KU-513-450

GRADED

FOR CHILDREN WITH MOTOR DIFFICULTIES

James P. Russell

Cambridge University Press

Cambridge

New York   New Rochelle

Melbourne   Sydney

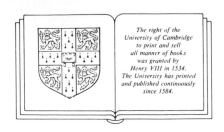

The right of the University of Cambridge to print and sell all manner of books was granted by Henry VIII in 1534. The University has printed and published continuously since 1584.

Published by the Press Syndicate of the University of Cambridge
The Pitt Building, Trumpington Street, Cambridge CB2 1RP
32 East 57th Street, New York, NY 10022, USA
10 Stamford Road, Oakleigh, Melbourne 3166, Australia

© Cambridge University Press 1988

First published 1988

Printed in Great Britain by Scotprint, Musselburgh, Scotland

British Library cataloguing in publication data

Russell, James P.
    Graded activities for children with motor
    difficulties.
    1. Motor ability in children   2. Teaching
    – Aid and devices
    I. Title
    155.4′12   BF723.M6

Library of Congress catalogue card number: 87-8011

ISBN 0 521 33852 2

DS

Designed by Right Angle Studios Ltd.

Graded activities for children with motor difficulties

CONTENTS

Acknowledgements

My professional colleagues, in schools and the advisory service, have all contributed in some way to this book. As I piloted the programmes with classes, groups and individuals I have valued and benefited greatly from comments and criticisms made by the teachers involved with the pupils on a day to day basis.

There are, however, some more sustained and systematic contributions which must be acknowledged. Fife Regional Council Education Committee and the Director of Education, Magnus More, have given me great encouragement and support throughout the project. Winifred Barclay and Helen Wilkie must be thanked for the help they gave me in the initial stages of writing and using the programmes. I am also indebted to Douglas McBride for providing the excellent art work. Finally I must acknowledge the contribution of Caroline Smith who took the manuscript through draft and redraft thoroughly, conscientiously and uncomplainingly.

FOREWORD

In many schools physical education is associated with the development of sporting excellence. Success enhances the prestige of the school and the status of the teacher. While there is a place for this, as it undoubtedly contributes to the personal development of the successful children involved, it does not meet the needs of children with motor learning difficulties. These children, sometimes referred to as 'clumsy' children, will gain in competence and self-esteem if they are offered an appropriate movement education programme in primary school. For this reason the developments in assisting children with motor learning problems being undertaken by Fife Regional Council's Education Department deserve wide notice.

Motor learning difficulties lie in the grey area between the remit of the teacher, the psychologist and the doctor. The teacher may feel ill-prepared to help the child with difficulties in dressing, writing or ball games. Psychologists lack convenient, valid and reliable tests of motor ability. Doctors face uncertainty when confronted by a child whose motor difficulties are not sufficient to indicate a specific disease. Yet motor learning problems have been shown to be a persistent characteristic associated with educational failure, social isolation, anxiety, withdrawal and depression persisting into adolescence. One solution is to seek the advice of physiotherapists or occupational therapists but such resources are scarce and not always prepared for clumsy children. However, therapists can often contribute advice or short-term treatment programmes.

There is a need for discussion and mutual education between interested professions to promote the understanding of such children and development of ideas of ways to help them. Acceptance of the problem by professionals, parents and children is the first step. Circumvention of obstacles is the second step. The third step is to consider ways of remediating the problem. Children tend to avoid activities they find difficult (as do we all), but if they believe that they will never succeed, they may not achieve their potential. It is not suggested that we should find what children do worst and make them practise these activities to the point of boredom. Nor is it suggested that everyone should achieve high standards in motor skills. But if children have movement difficulties, they may be grateful for the opportunity to improve or to find activities in which they can succeed. Though improvement of movement education may require more resources it has been shown that involvement of parents and older pupils in the school movement education programme can be beneficial for all concerned.

A welcome feature of this book is its recognition of the diversity of children with motor problems. Some have motor planning difficulty, some know what they want to do but their fingers won't work properly, others have poor balance. It is quite possible to be good at jigsaws or drawing and to have illegible handwriting. (I have met a teenage boy who temporarily lost the ability to read following a severe attack of migraine. After writing a page to dictation at normal speed and without mistakes he was unable to read it back. Such inconsistencies seem baffling but are explicable from our knowledge of how the brain works.) It is likely that accurate assessment of individual children and development of appropriate educational plans will be easier to evaluate than global packages for 'typical' clumsy children. The varied and progressive nature of the programmes described here offers a means to that end.

Motor learning and literacy difficulties are separate issues in general. However they do co-exist in individual children, placing them at considerable disadvantage. It is more common for co-ordination (including handwriting) and maths difficulties to go together. Do movement education programmes lead to better literacy, numeracy, handwriting or motor competence? It is justified to make the attempt and create the opportunity to evaluate them. Success could come from a direct effect of teaching or from a broader effect on the child's willingness to 'have a go'. More accurate perception of what sort of a child he or she *is* will be achieved by taking motor skills into account. Perhaps each school should have a staff member who knows how to look at a child with educational or behaviour problems in this way. It is satisfying for *staff* to come to understand such children better.

This book is a resource for those who want to help such children while they are still young. It offers structure to movement education programmes suitable for these diverse, interesting and rewarding children who have so often fallen between the experts' stools.

Ian McKinlay
Consultant Paediatric Neurologist
University of Manchester School of Medicine

INTRODUCTION

Why this book was written

In recent years there has been an increasing emphasis on assisting pupils with learning difficulties and within this area of education there are many children with motor difficulties. In secondary schools, teachers of Physical Education are well placed and equipped to assist pupils with motor learning difficulties, but there are comparatively few Physical Education specialist teachers in Primary and Special Schools. The pupils are dependent on the help which can be given to them by class or remedial teachers.

Who this book is for

This book has been produced to assist both the class and remedial teachers in the Special and Primary sectors of education. It has been devised to help those teachers who have little or no specialist training in Physical Education but who may be required to work with pupils to help them with their motor problems. It will also be of value to Primary and Nursery staff, Occupational Therapists and those in charge of Mother and Toddler groups.

The objectives of this book

1 To allow pupils with motor difficulties to achieve success. This has been done by grading the activities in each programme according to their degree of difficulty so that pupils using them can be placed at their own levels of achievement and thus enjoy the activity.

2 To allow pupils to succeed, progress and to perceive clearly their own level of progress. This has been achieved by breaking down basic motor activities to their simplest components.

3 To prepare activities which the non-specialist teacher (in Physical Education terms) would be able to understand and use.

4 To devise activities which can be used in small areas when a gymnasium is not available and which use simple basic equipment which most schools have readily available.

Children and learning difficulties

The activities are aimed at two types of pupils with motor difficulties.

1 Pupils with academic learning problems who also have what would appear to be related motor problems.

2 Children who have been diagnosed as having only motor problems and require some special help to overcome their problems.

The pupil with academic learning problems

Reading and writing are extremely complex skills involving the integration of numerous components of both a physical and an intellectual nature.

Children, when they first attend nursery or infant school, are usually given a pre-reading and pre-writing programme and the elements contained in them are recognised as essential pre-requisites to the acquisition of these skills. The following list contains **some** of the pre-requisites and will be referred to throughout the text as the **Techniques List.**

Techniques List
- Listening/talking
- Vocabulary
- Auditory and visual sequential memory
- Visual discrimination/perception
- Gross motor control
- Fine motor control
- Balance
- Body awareness
- Spatial awareness
- Co-ordination
- The ability to distinguish between left and right
- Visual tracking
- Rhythm

It is clear that the vast majority of the items on the list are of a physical nature. Attempting and gaining mastery of them through *physical* movement should afford the child considerable help in the learning processes which take place as the skills are acquired.

Skills and Techniques Having used the words 'skill' and 'techniques' it may be useful to distinguish between the two and I should like to use the analogy of games coaching.

Technique is the ability to perform a single action, e.g. heading or kicking a ball, striking a ball with a racquet.
Skill is the ability to use that technique or single action consistently well in the appropriate situation during the full game.
If a child can master the components of the Technique List – the single

actions – he or she can come to use them automatically and thus be able to concentrate on the intellectual components of reading and writing – the full game – without *physical* distractions.

The elements of the Techniques List are important for very young children but it must be stressed that attainment of them remains important throughout the learning process. However, some children who have received several years of post-five education are observed by their class teachers to continue to have difficulties with reading and writing. If the problems are severe the child is referred to educational psychologists so that the reasons for the difficulties may be diagnosed. It is virtually certain that the diagnosis will light upon lack of one or more of the items on the Techniques List as possible contributary factors to the problems.

Remediation for the diagnosed physical elements can now be applied and a later assessment made of any improvement in acquiring the skills.

This remediation process is one concern of the programmes which follow. Obviously, though, *prevention* is preferable to *remediation* and the contention can be made that if the skills from the programme are used for young children, at least some of them may clear the hurdles of reading and writing with much greater ease.

Pre-reading vocabulary

Strictly speaking, a pre-reading vocabulary is not a technique but it is one component without which the printed page would be meaningless. With no picture or concept to put to a word the child cannot begin to comprehend. Learning a pre-reading vocabulary is closely interwoven with self, movement and cultural background. A child is taught to recognise body parts, clothing, gross motor actions, understand spatial and directional words, seriation, colour – *all of which are integral parts of any well-constructed programme of physical education*, therefore in a sense, a learned technique.

The child with motor difficulties but with no difficulties with academic subjects

Children in Special Schools, Special Units and those who have been referred to paediatricians and educational psychologists are in some ways fortunate because their motor problems will be diagnosed through approved tests and provision made for their alleviation.

The awkward child who has no other learning problems but who drops things; bumps into objects; doesn't write neatly; has difficulty with fine skills like tying shoe-laces; and cannot play games; may, as a result, go through school life without any special attention, when in fact a systematic programme of physical remediation might do much to help him or her.

The child with inefficient motor function may drop out of any form of physical activity, even at an early age. At worst he or she may display or develop a variety of symptoms such as inappropriate behaviour, anxiety, depression, aggression or be unduly timid and dependent. If the teacher is concerned advice should be sought.

A word of caution!

It is all too easy to label children and if a child with motor problems, who is perfectly well adjusted, happy, carefree and doing well academically, is suddenly withdrawn from class for special movement training, it may have adverse effects. Care must be taken to ensure that intervention is not interfering with the normal development of a happy, well-adjusted pupil.

Assessing the pupils with motor difficulties

Very few pupils are given special motor programmes unless they have been assessed by someone knowledgeable in tests and testing techniques. In the case of Special Education and children with learning difficulties or behavioural problems in mainstream Primary Education, assessment is made by school medical officers or psychologists who may diagnose some of the problems as similar to the items in the Techniques List. The assessment is the starting point and when a diagnosis is made certain measures may then be prescribed to try to overcome the problem.

Identifying the pupil with motor difficulties

How can you tell that a child without academic difficulties, has motor problems?

The following questions are useful *initially* in identifying a need for help.

1 Are the child's movements awkward, ungainly or cumbersome?
2 Is the child always slow to move?
3 Does the child frequently bump into people or things?
4 Does the child frequently drop things?
5 Does the child have difficulty with his/her balance or balancing items?
6 Does the child often fall over?
7 Does the child show a lack of movement skill?
8 Is their muscular development unable to control their bulk?

If the answer to most of these questions is yes, this might suggest that the appropriate member of staff should be notified and a decision made as to whether to take the matter further. This is particularly the case if the child is also noted to have other symptoms such as behavioural problems, is attention seeking, disruptive or withdrawn. The educational psychologist or school medical officer is well placed to advise on what is causing the motor difficulty and their diagnosis will almost certainly show items similar to those in the Techniques List. The psychologist may also give advice on whether or not the child should be placed on a special movement programme. Once the assessment is given to the school the teacher can select the appropriate programme for the pupil.

There is absolutely no point in a psychologist only reporting to the school that a child requires balance activities, co-ordination work, or ball handling. Non-specialist teachers (in physical education terms) need prescriptive programmes to which they can refer.

Observations on working with children with motor problems

It must be said that children with motor problems (especially those with academic learning difficulties also) require as much tolerance, sympathy, understanding and encouragement with their efforts as possible.

The normal class Physical Education lesson of one or two periods per week in a Primary school does not always help children with motor problems. They cannot get the degree of attention they need because all members of the class have calls on the teacher's time. The class lesson may even be disadvantageous to them. Repeated failure, in front of their peers, to match normal expected performance of skills in the lesson, produces and gradually hardens an attitude of failure. They 'can't play'; nobody wants to dance with them; they are never chosen or are last to be chosen for teams; classmates laugh at their inability to cope. This situation reinforces their feelings of inadequacy and their self-esteem and self-image are destroyed.

Another disadvantage of the class PE lesson may be the method of presentation of work. In the main an *exploratory* approach is used. Children with motor problems benefit from the stage by stage progression of a *prescriptive* type of approach until skill and self-confidence are gained and they are ready to participate with their classmates without fear of ridicule.

For children with academic learning difficulties the programmes of physical activities may not be the panacea for all ills. However the Techniques List shows there is more to helping those children than 'sitting at a desk' remedies. This physical input should be part of multisensory activity programmes which would also include music, drama and art.

It should be noted that children who are good at games but who have problems with reading, writing or both can also benefit from a remedial motor programme. For example, a good netball player may have fine motor control or auditory sequential memory problems. This child's love of activity can be channelled into using the activities from the appropriate programme to help overcome the problem.

All teachers, both class and specialist PE teachers, should be made more aware of the stages of physical development in children, the possibilities offered in the normal PE lesson for language development and also the contribution of physical education to learning in its broadest sense.

As has already been indicated all the programmes should be seen as a *resource* for helping children with motor problems rather like this analogy:

> If you have a locked door in your house and the key to that door has been lost, the greater the variety of keys you can collect to try to unlock the door, the more chance there is of finding one which will work.

The programmes are an educational key. I would urge teachers, parents and therapists to try this key. I am confident that its use will give to children beneficial, pleasurable and confidence-building experiences which they can carry outside the classroom and integrate into their patterns of life.

The programmes

Some of the children may be suffering from lack of achievement in *all* curriculum activities. The activities in each programme are graded from easy to more difficult, to substitute experiences of genuine achievement for all children, for experience of failure, no matter how great their motor difficulties may be. Because of the progressive nature of the activities the teacher is able to recognise achievement easily and react positively to it.

It should be recognised that even the finest-meshed remedial net may fail to pick up pupils who need help. Each programme represents a systematic approach which should allow non-specialist teachers to operate remedial activities which can be seen by the pupils as part of ordinary PE activity. Pupils with motor difficulties who follow the programmes can thus begin to participate in a physical education lesson, games or just everyday play with their peer group, without feeling inadequate.

Which programmes and activities should be used?

The key to any programme is the very low level starting point for each activity — a low level of starting point which nevertheless attracts and holds the interest of the pupil. This is coupled to a very gradual increase in degree of difficulty throughout a programme.

As far as possible the activities have been categorised under the headings from the Techniques List. This will allow the teacher to select an activity from the appropriate programme with which the pupil will succeed, then progress. The selection should be carried out on a trial and error basis.

It should be noted that a number of the programmes overlap (see Techniques breakdown); Gross Motor Work and Body Awareness are in the Visual Tracking programme (page 78); Auditory Sequential Memory is in the Balance programme (page 37); listening is common to all programmes. Consequently a variety of different types of work can be undertaken for the same problem. In the overlapping programmes the teacher can emphasise the area of difficulty he or she particularly wants to help. See Table 1 at the end of this introduction.

How to use the programmes effectively

1 The activities may be given to individuals or small groups.
2 They may be taught in a gym or any available small area.
3 They may be used as a group activity in the normal PE programme set out especially for the pupils with a difficulty.
4 The normal format of a PE lesson is:
   (a) Introductory movement,
   (b) Movement training,
   (c) Group work.

This same format may be used for taking a small group of children by selecting activities from programmes appropriate to the problems of the children concerned. If there are a number of children requiring assistance they should be taken in groups of *no more than six pupils*. This allows the teacher to observe and assist each child.

How to prepare a group programme

1 Select the areas of difficulty most common to the group and use items from the appropriate programme for Introductory activities and Movement training.

2 Look at the remaining areas of difficulty being experienced by the children and select activities from programmes which are appropriate to these as items for group training, then direct the children to these specific groups.

How to make use of Pupil Profiles

The following are examples of typical Pupil Profiles supplied by Child Guidance and from these, areas of need can be identified and lessons prepared accordingly, using whichever methods of presenting the activities are appropriate to the school or situation.

Pupil 1
right-handed
right-footed
right-eyed
right-eared

Problems
short concentration span - impulsive and erratic - easily distracted - orientation - auditory sequential memory - body awareness.

Pupil 2
left-handed
left-footed
left-eyed

Problems
oldest of seven - 362 absences in first two years of schooling - (at age 7½) 'has not attained pre-reading skills' - friendly - exhibitionist

Pupil 3
left-handed
right-footed
right-eyed

Problems
background - elder of twins - hyperactive - impulsive, extremely poor concentration - unable to take things slowly - visual motor perception - fine motor skills - auditory sequencing - visual sequencing - rhythm.

Pupil 4
right-handed
right-footed
left-eyed
weak left arm

Problems
background - (at age 5½) very withdrawn. Because of severe visual, auditory and motor problems he could not participate in many of the classroom activities. Raised voices made him physically ill. Criticism led to further withdrawal. (At age 7½) anxious to succeed, frightened to make mistakes - very poor gross/fine motor control.
(At age 8) much more communicative, but still physically shakes when presented with a new problem. Unable to respond to verbal instructions (no kinaesthetic sense). Visual sequencing - auditory sequencing - sound blending - sound discrimination - rhythm - gross motor - fine motor - poor body image.

I would suggest, for example, that in the case of *Pupil 3* an individual programme of work would be arranged as follows.

Introductory activity   —   Items from Programmes 2, 7, 12.
Movement training   —   Items from Programmes 4, 12, 13.

If schools are to be involved in helping children with motor problems it is important that Headteachers and Assistant Headteachers be made aware of the implications of the problems and the value of motor remediation. The staff may also have to convince parents involved that the motor programmes given to their child are integral parts of the remedial approach.

The placing of a child on any programme of remediation can sometimes carry with it the stigma of being of low ability and consequently of low worth. While parents can often be convinced that remedial help with numeracy and literacy can benefit their child, they often need more convincing about the need for motor training in this same area of education. They may not even be convinced of the value of it for the child with only motor problems!

Staff in schools using the programme must thoroughly verse themselves in the rationale behind motor remediation so that they can convince the parents of its worth. Even if the belief that links exist between poor motor control and poor literacy and numeracy is far from current throughout the profession, strong subjective professional opinions of teachers who have used the programmes should encourage teachers to proceed with them, on the grounds that, at the very least, they improve greatly the self-image and confidence of the child with motor problems.

How parents can help

Those concerned with education know that the vocabulary section of a Pre-reading programme is vitally important if a child is to get off to a good start in reading.

This chapter can be recommended as a *learning package* to parents of young children who may wish to use constructive teaching and learning approaches in the home. It does not interfere with any teaching methodology but will have benefits for the child in school.

Parents may not know exactly what a child is expected to know before they can read, but many of them try to help their children and try to glean information on how to do this from a variety of sources. The best advice to parents on how to prepare their children for reading is **PLAY WITH THEM**.

The relevance of the advice on Pre-reading vocabulary may be seen in the approach advocated in the use of the programme. The children's play is structured to give them familiarity and knowledge of certain words and phrases.

Learning new words in a Pre-reading programme is best done by experiencing what the words mean. Through the experience the meaning of the word is learned and understood. Reading is the reconstruction of meaning: the meaning is not in print. That comes from experience and is gained by 'doing'.

> 'Read it — forget it'
> 'Write it — remember it'
> 'Do it and *know* it'

If the basic words and phrases are not experienced the children find difficulty not only in learning to read but in following simple instructions in class.

Vocabulary   Before they can read children are expected to understand, be able to recognise and to have experience of words that are required for daily living.

1 **Body parts**   Every part must be known from head to toe, including such parts as eyebrows, fingernails, knuckles, palms, elbows, stomach, etc.
2 **Clothing**   Every item which a child wears must be known and the child able to name it: skirt, tie, trousers, wellingtons, shirt, blouse, etc.
3 **Objects**   at home, in school and the classroom. Parents must concern themselves with teaching the names of objects at home.
4 **Gross motor actions**   These are activities involving big body movements and children should 'experience' them and be able to recognise other children carrying out these actions: walk, run, crawl, climb, sit, roll, tiptoe, stretch, curl, twist, turn, stop, start, hit, push, pull, jump, land, skip, hop, etc.
5 **Spatial relationships**   Simply put it means that a child should know where he or she is in space and how he or she relates to objects around or near him or her.
   (a) *Directions*: up, down, over, under, through, up through, down through, to the right, to the left, left, right, forward, backwards, sideways, etc.
   (b) *Position*: inside, outside, on, in, near, far, over, under, between, top, bottom, high, low, there, here, across, back to back, side by side, in front of, etc.
6 **Categories**   Words concerned with size, speed, consistency, e.g. similarity, difference, opposite, slow, fast, quick, bit, little, small, tall, fat, thin, high, low, different, same, wide, narrow, hard, soft, etc.
7 **Comparatives and superlatives**   Slower, slowest, quicker, quickest, higher, highest, low, lowest, fast, faster, fastest, etc.

To become used to the language and how to use it in play, write out lists of words and phrases under the appropriate headings and make up activities for the children. After this has been done a number of times there is little need for it as it becomes artificial. It does make the parent conscious of the words children can absorb when playing and they begin to introduce appropriate words in *spontaneous play situations*.

Activities   **Gross motor actions**

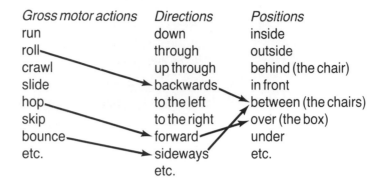

Gross motor actions	*Directions*	*Positions*
run	down	inside
roll	through	outside
crawl	up through	behind (the chair)
slide	backwards	in front
hop	to the left	between (the chairs)
skip	to the right	over (the box)
bounce	forward	under
etc.	sideways	etc.
	etc.	

The motor actions are 'played at' first then they are used with a directional or positional word or both as the children become more proficient and are seen to understand the words. Parents may also participate by performing some of the activities while the children are asked 'what', 'where' and 'how' questions.

Knowledge of body parts and body awareness

When learning the body parts children should be asked to touch them, name them and find out how they relate to each other. Being able to touch and name body parts on the *opposite* side of the mid line of the body and do it accurately is important.

Children should also be able to name and recognise not only their own body parts but those of others. They should have practice in doing this not only while standing but in *any* position, e.g. lying on their sides, fronts, backs, upside down.

They should also be schooled to touch and name parts they cannot see, e.g. bottom, shoulder blade, back. When their eyes are closed they must be able to touch all named body parts.

When a parent is playing wrestling for example, questions could be asked of the child when he or she is in many positions.

> 'Where is your nose?'
> 'Hold my left hand'
> 'Put your left leg round my waist, hold it with your right hand'.

If the child is unsure of the name the parent should touch firmly the appropriate body part and name it. The child is asked to name it immediately and then asked again later. This is known as tactile feedback as the child may still have the sensation of touch in that particular body part.

Singing games are another obvious, enjoyable method of training body awareness and should be used frequently. Through this, awareness of rhythm is increased.

Listening skills and auditory memory

Listening skills are being practised when a short sequence of instructions is given and the child is then asked to carry out the instructions.

Roll across the carpet *in front of* your Mummy.
Stand *behind* the couch then *hop towards* the door.

While these skills are being taught, parents should be aware of any *new* words they might wish to introduce and check that the children are acting out these words correctly.

Tuck your head in.
Curl up into a ball.
Stretch out as you roll over sideways.

Categories
The words concerned with size, difference, opposites and similarities can be reproduced, e.g.

roll quietly; hop softly; put your feet wide apart.

Language development using a ball
(a) Possible new words and phrases:

pat	balance	aim	toss
bounce	partner	throw	bowl
keep up	target	spin	underarm

(b) Possible words and phrases used when teaching the gross actions,

e.g. throwing a ball.
   Hold the ball *firmly* in the fingers.
   Stand *sideways, one foot in front of the other.*

(c) Listening skills, e.g. throw the ball gently to me, run round behind me then run back to the wall.

The possibilities are endless for children learning words and their meaning through play. Parents must make themselves fully aware of what they are doing and how vital a role they can play in this aspect of education. Vast sums of money are paid in the purchase of 'educational toys' and they do have their place. It is of vital importance, however, that parents come to realise that the best toys exist in the learning experiences through fun and play which interested adults can use to increase children's knowledge and enrich their lives.

Table 1   A breakdown of techniques covered by more than one programme.

TECHNIQUES	INTRODUCTION	PROG 1	PROG 2	PROG 3	PROG 4	PROG 5	PROG 6	PROG 7	PROG 8	PROG 9	PROG 10	PROG 11	PROG 12	PROG 13	PROG 14
	How parents can help	Gross motor co-ordination	Gross motor control walking/running	Dynamic balance	Balance/hopping/skipping	Catching	Striking/kicking	Jumping	Body awareness	Knowledge of left & right	Activities involving left & right movements	Visual discrimination	Visual tracking	Activities for the writing hand	Establishing hand writing patterns
Listening/talking	X	X	X	X	X	X	X	X	X	X	X	X	X	X	X
Vocabulary	X	X	X	X	X	X	X	X	X	X	X	X	X	X	X
Auditory and visual sequential memory	X	X			X			X	X			X			
Visual discrimination Perception	X	X	X			X	X	X		X		X	X		X
Gross motor control	X	X	X	X	X	X	X	X	X	X	X	X	X	X	X
Gross motor approaching fine and fine motor control					X						X			X	X
Balance	X	X		X	X		X	X	X			X	X		X
Body awareness	X	X			X	X	X		X			X	X	X	
Spatial awareness	X	X	X			X						X			
Co-ordination	X		X	X	X	X				X	X		X	X	X
Knowledge of left and right	X		X	X	X		X		X	X	X		X	X	X
Visual tracking			X	X	X	X	X			X		X	X		
Rhythm	X			X								X			

Gross motor control and co-ordination

This programme incorporates:
- **body awareness**
- **visual perception work**
- **motor planning**
- **auditory sequential memory**
- **visual sequential memory**

The activities in this programme are for children with gross motor problems and elementary language difficulties. They require elements of co-ordination, and can be used to extend the children's vocabulary as part of a Pre-reading programme.

Stepping over obstacles

Activities

Equipment needed
Arcade activity skittles, canes and hoops.

1 Step *over* canes placed on the ground.

2 Step *over* canes supported on skittles at ankle height.

3 Step *over* canes at calf height.

4 Step *over* canes at knee height.

5 Step *over* canes at slightly above knee height.

6 A mixture of 1, 2, 3, 4 and 5.

Notes

Each of these activities can be made progressively more difficult as follows:

(i) Place the canes 1 m apart and parallel.

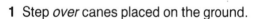

(ii) Place the canes close together and parallel.

(iii) Place the canes at an angle to each other.

(iv) Canes, supported on skittles, crossing at various heights.

(v) Use hoops, parallel to the floor, supported by skittles.

Extending the vocabulary of position and movement

Activities

Equipment needed

Arcade activity skittles; canes; hoops; flashcards.

1 Step *over* and crawl *under* canes alternately. (Place the canes below knee height for stepping over, and above knee height for crawling under.)

2 As in 1, but place the canes at the same height.

3 Move *over* and *under* canes, then *through* a hoop.

4 As in 3, but alter the order of instructions, e.g. *through, over, under*.

5 Place a hoop or hoops on skittles, parallel to the floor, together with the canes. The instructions can then be extended to include *under* or *through* the hoop, or *up through* or *down through* the hoop.

6 Moving *over* and *under* canes, *through* a hoop and *between* skittles.

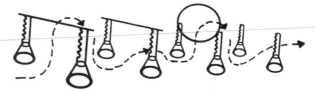

7 As in 6, but add hoops parallel to the ground. The instructions can then be given as in 5.

8 As in 6 and 7, but change the order of the activities.

Notes

(i) The degree of difficulty for each activity can be increased by placing the apparatus as follows:
far apart
close together
zig-zag pattern
varying the heights of the canes or hoops

(ii) Ask the children to go head first or feet first, on their backs or their fronts, at the through/under/between stages.

(iii) Children should be asked to name the part of the body which touches or knocks down the apparatus. If they cannot name the body parts, hold or touch firmly the part of the body which touched the apparatus, asking the child to name it immediately. Do this again at the end of the activity. The tactile feedback from the firm touch will reinforce the child's memory.

(iv) To increase the children's awareness and interest, tie small bells (as for budgerigar cages) to canes and hoops, and then ask them to move under/over, etc. without ringing bells.

(v) Ask children to repeat the sequence to give them practice in auditory or visual recall.

(vi) Use flashcards –
OVER
UNDER
THROUGH
BETWEEN
UP THROUGH
DOWN THROUGH
– to show the sequence of instructions.

(1) Vary the sequences.

(2) Remove the cards: ask pupils to repeat the sequence.

(3) One child sets out a sequence of flashcard instructions. Another child carries out the instructions, the first child checking that each part of the sequence is done correctly.

(4) One child makes up his or her own sequence on the apparatus, while another responds by laying down the appropriate flashcards.

PROGRAMME 2

Gross motor control – walking and running

This programme includes elements of:
- **visual perception**
- **motor planning**

Walking and running are fundamental skills which, of all the gross motor activities, children must master for everyday living.

Because they are so basic and because most children can walk and run, albeit many of them not well, teachers tend to ignore *teaching* anything about them. These skills are taken for granted and teachers hope that the pupils can play games and walk through crowded classrooms or corridors without bumping into people or things. If they do knock things over, the comment is made that the children are clumsy and it is left at that.

Walking and running require good balance, co-ordination, visual perception and motor planning; if children do not have these abilities, they can be presented with a variety of graded activities to help them to cope better.

For example, a group of children walking or running at the same time in restricted space helps them to develop their peripheral vision. Introducing items on the ground and in the air, such as school bags and balloons, allows children to practise looking down and up as well as in a wide horizontal plane. This development of peripheral vision, apart from being a prerequisite of efficient games playing, is essential for the children's safety when walking along busy streets or cycling in traffic. Through training they become more conscious of what is happening around them and can react more quickly.

WALKING ACTIVITIES

Children should be exposed to a wide variety of experiences in walking: changing direction; walking on different surfaces; moving between obstacles; carrying boxes which they cannot easily see over or round; carrying long or heavy objects.

When coaching walking, use simple instructions to improve children's posture: for example, 'Walk tall!', 'Pull your head up!'

Do not be over-concerned about the arm swing. If you mention this, the children having problems may experience anxiety because of their inability to co-ordinate arm and leg actions. Ask them simply to allow their arms to hang loosely – they will often begin to swing their arms naturally.

Look for smooth, fluid walking, without stiffness or jerkiness.

It is advantageous to start with the foot-strengthening activities given in programme 3. The following activities can then be used.

Activities

1 Walk towards a fixed point some distance away.

2 Walk along a straight line marked in the playground or gym.

3 Walk along court markings in the playground or gym.

4 Walk, turning left, right or about-turning to command. (NB. This should not be military-style marching!)

5 Walk, changing direction frequently.

6 Walk straight forward but turn the upper body to left or right, on request.

7 Perform the above activities walking on different parts of the feet, heels, toes, outside and inside.

At this point practise balance walking on different surfaces (see programme 3).

Obstacle work

Equipment needed

Classroom furniture; large and small PE equipment; cardboard boxes of different sizes and shapes, with string round them; plastic shopping bags containing a variety of objects; trays or boards; empty tins; plastic cups; washing-up liquid bottles.

Preparation

Construct a small obstacle course using a variety of PE or classroom equipment. Ropes or the backs of chairs may be used to form narrow passages. Include changes of direction in the course. Small budgerigar bells can be hung at strategic places to increase the fun!

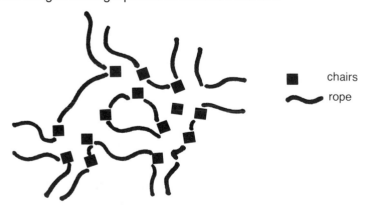

■ chairs

∿ rope

Activities

1 Walk through the course, in the ways described in activities 4, 5, 6 and 7 of the previous section.

2 As in 1, carrying a box by the string in one hand. Plastic shopping bags can also be carried.

3 As in 1, carrying two boxes by the string, one in each hand. Vary the size of the boxes, and have a different size of box in each hand.

4 As in 1, carrying a variety of sizes and shapes of boxes, one at a time, in both hands. (See note (v) below.)

5 As in 1, carrying a tray or board in two hands on which is placed a small box or boxes.

6 As in 5, but with an empty tin/tins, plastic cup/cups or washing-up liquid bottles on the tray.

7 As in 1, holding in one hand a table tennis bat on which is balanced a bean bag.

8 As in 7, but balancing a shuttlecock on its feather tips on the bat.

9 As in 7, but balancing a shuttlecock on its side on the bat.

10 As in 7, but balancing an aerflo ball on the bat.

11 Divide the group into two. Half walks through the course without carrying anything, the other half carries various pieces of equipment while they walk.

12 When the children can achieve good walking and carrying, place a variety of items on the ground throughout the course, e.g. school bags, small boxes, waste paper bins, etc.

Notes

(i) For each activity initially ask a single child to walk through the course, giving them a starting and a finishing point. Gradually ask more children to walk through the course at the same time. Have each child start and finish at different points so that they must meet and pass somewhere within the course.

(ii) Children should avoid touching the obstacles or anyone else with their bodies or with any object they are carrying. If they do touch anything, ask them which part of their body touched it. If they are unable to do this, touch or hold the part firmly and ask them to name it. Repeat the question when they have completed the course.

(iii) When articles are carried through narrow gaps, emphasise the 'body turning' movement needed: i.e. turning the upper body sideways while walking forward (see activity 6 above).

(iv) The activities can be played as a game, as follows. Ask the children to walk a given pathway without touching any obstacle. If they complete the course without touching any obstacles, give them 10 points. Deduct 1 point each time an obstacle is touched.

(v) Activity 4 provides an opportunity of teaching children how to carry a large object using both hands. The following points are worth emphasising.

(1) To avoid strain, the hands should hold the object at different levels.

(2) The object should be lifted higher than is strictly necessary to carry it.

(3) If the object is brought to the body and lowered against the child's *clothing*, the friction between the box and the clothing will help to keep the box in position. The child's shoulder will take some of the weight through the clothing, making it easier for the child to hold the object for long periods.

RUNNING ACTIVITIES

Children need to be able to run for a variety of reasons. They may need to run to get somewhere quickly, perhaps through crowded streets, carrying cases or shopping bags; and, of course, running is involved in most games.

Running is very seldom done in a straight line. When frequent changes of direction, dodging obstacles, and stopping quickly are required, the right kind of footwork is vital to maintain balance. For example, it is important that children's feet do not cross or even come close together when the children turn or stop; otherwise, it is difficult for the children to maintain body balance or push off in another direction.

Stopping **Teaching points**

(i) Both feet should hit the ground almost simultaneously when stopping. To help children become aware of this, give the command to stop as 'Stop, 1, 2' (say this *quickly*). Ask the children to listen to their feet slapping down on the 1, 2 count.

(ii) The feet should be kept apart. One foot – the 'braking foot' – will land slightly in front of the other.

(iii) Knees should be bent slightly on stopping. This can be achieved by the children lowering their bottoms, as if about to sit. The faster the children are running, the further down their bottoms need to be lowered.

Equipment needed
Hoops

Activities

1 Practise the 'bottom down', knees slightly bent position, while standing.

2 Children run slowly across the room in a line, and stop on command, trying to lower their bottoms quickly.

3 As in 2, using the command 'Stop, 1, 2'. Take time to make sure this is understood.

4 As in 3, but gradually increasing the running speed.

5 Place hoops in a line half way up the room. Children run and stop when they reach a hoop. Gradually increase the running speed.

6 (In pairs.) One child from each pair stands in a hoop. The other runs up to and stops – on the command 'Stop, 1, 2' – in front of his or her partner.

7 As in 6, with no command.

8 (In pairs.) Children start from opposite sides of the room, run towards their partner and stop in the correct position facing each other. They then pass and continue running to the other side of the room.

9 As in 8, but stop facing partner, turn round and run back to the starting point.

Changing direction

Teaching points

(i) Feet should be apart.

(ii) Knees are slightly bent, and the bottom slightly lowered.

(iii) Movement sideways is a 'gliding' type of movement. Feet move quickly, close to the ground. Legs never cross or come together.

(iv) Push off hard with the left foot if changing direction to the right, and vice versa.

Equipment needed
Hoops; large balls; classroom furniture and large PE equipment; cardboard boxes used in obstacle work.

Activities

1 Children practise the feet apart, bottom lowered, knees slightly bent stance, and 'glide' sideways to left or right.

2 As in 1, with the teacher calling out the direction.

3 (In pairs.) Partners face each other, feet apart. One from each pair moves sideways to the left and the right, changing direction frequently. The other tries to move so that they always face their partner.

4 (In pairs.) One from each pair 'defends' a hoop by standing outside it. The other tries to dodge past, trying to place a foot in the hoop. Watch the footwork.

5 Scatter large balls and hoops on the floor. Children run between the balls without touching them. When they run to a hoop, they dodge past it using the appropriate footwork.

6 (In pairs.) One child follows the other. The child in front dodges from side to side as they move forward. The child behind attempts to stay close behind their partner by dodging in the same direction.

7 All children run and dodge past each other. Begin to restrict the area in which they are running.

8 Place a variety of larger equipment on the floor: chairs, desks, mats, PE trestles etc. Children run between the apparatus without touching it.

9 As in 8, carrying a large ball cradled in the arms.

10 As in 9, carrying a large ball under each arm.

11 As in 10, carrying a box in one hand (see activity 2 of 'Obstacle work').

12 As in 11, carrying boxes in both hands.

Developing peripheral vision

Equipment needed
Balloons of different colours.

1 Children run in any direction looking at the teacher all the time but avoiding bumping into others. (Remind children not to cross their feet if they have to move sideways.)

2 Children run in any direction. Knock a balloon into the air and ask the children to keep running, but to watch the balloon until it touches the ground.

3 As in 2, but children stop and sit down as soon as the balloon touches the ground.

4 Children run in any direction. Quickly knock a number of balloons into the air, one at a time. Ask the children to continue running, and to call out the colour of each balloon as it hits the ground. When the last balloon lands, the children should stop and sit down.

P R O G R A M M E	3

Dynamic balance programme

This programme incorporates:
- **gross motor work**
- **foot/eye co-ordination**
- **hand/eye co-ordination**
- **sequential memory skills**

Dynamic balance is concerned with maintaining good postural control while moving. This type of control may be very difficult for a child with motor problems.

Children need to be exposed to a variety of situations in which they can practise postural control, remembering that not all surfaces on which they move will be flat or stable.

An important feature of children's balance is the ability to use their feet to grip the surface on which they are moving. If different surfaces and textures are provided, their awareness of this will be increased, while at the same time the muscles and tendons of their feet will be strengthened. Accordingly, children should perform balance activities using bare feet.

The notes at the end of the programme are important for challenging the pupils.

STRENGTHENING FEET AND ANKLES

Equipment needed
PE bench; tennis balls; coloured PE bands; pencils, rubbers, sacks, plastic cups, etc.

1 Walk on different parts of the feet – toes, heels, outsides and insides.

2 As in 1, changing direction frequently; e.g. follow lines on the floor, move in and out of the obstacles, etc.

3 As in 1, moving forwards, backwards and sideways.

4 Sit on a bench and roll a tennis ball, in all directions, under the left foot, the right foot, then both feet together.

5 Sit on a bench and pick up coloured PE bands by gripping with the toes. Use both feet.

6 As in 5, picking up a variety of objects, e.g. pencils, rubbers, plastic cups, socks, etc.

7 As in 5, but standing, using left and right feet to pick up the bands. Ask children to try to balance on one leg for a few seconds while holding the band. Emphasise the 'gripping' action of the *standing* foot.

8 As in 6, but standing. Lift objects with one foot, hop on other.

9 Kneel with toes and heels touching – sit on heels. Bounce gently on the heels to a given rhythm.

10 (In pairs.) Sit facing a partner, legs straight out with soles of the feet against soles of partner's feet. One child pushes with their toes, keeping their heels on the ground. The other allows their toes to be pushed back.

Games **Equipment needed**

Coloured PE bands; waste paper baskets; watch; pencils, socks, plastic cups, etc.

1 (In groups of two or more.) Group sits on a bench. Put a pile of coloured PE bands and a waste paper basket in front of each child. The children use their left or right feet to lift as many bands into the basket as possible within a given time. The winner is the child with most bands in their basket.

2 As in 1, using a variety of articles, e.g. pencils, bands, socks, plastic cups, etc.

3 Move the waste paper baskets a short distance away from the children. The children pick up an item (as in 1 or 2), hop to the basket, run back and collect another item. The winner is the first child to place all the objects in their basket.

Notes

(i) Before attempting games with 'winners' allow children to become familiar with the activity, for example by timing how long it takes to lift six bands. Next they attempt to beat their own time.

(ii) These games may be used for

   (1) *Colour identification* – e.g. pick up only green bands.
   (2) *Sequencing* – e.g. pick up 1 red band, 2 blue bands and then a paper cup.

BALANCE WALKING

Using a variety of surfaces

Equipment needed
Recticel gym mats; bean bags; small balls; ropes; cut-out paper footprints.

Activities

1 Put Recticel gym mats in a line. Children walk along the row of mats – forwards, backwards, sideways.

2 Turn Recticel mats upside down to expose the honeycomb surface. Children walk along the mats – forwards, backwards, sideways.

3 As in 1 and 2, with bean bags, knotted ropes, small balls, etc. placed under the mats to make the surface *uneven*.

4 Children walk between two ropes or lines – normally, on toes, sideways, backwards, forwards. Start with the ropes about 50cm apart. As the children progress put the ropes closer together.

5 As in activity 4, placing the ropes on the row of mats with the uneven surface (see activity 3).

6 Put cut-out footprint patterns on the uneven surfaced mats.

7 Walk along a rope using the following patterns:
(i) straight pathway, (ii) curved pathway, (iii) zig-zag pathway, (iv) variety of pathways.

8 Place bean bags in a walking pattern in a line. Children walk on the bean bags.

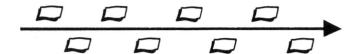

9 As in 8, bean bags placed in line. Use the following patterns: (i) a straight line, (ii) a curved pattern, (iii) a zig-zag pattern.

Using more difficult apparatus

Equipment needed

Two balancing planks; bean bags; ropes; small PE mats; PE bench; ladder.

Sequence for each activity

Ask the children to perform this sequence in each of the activities below.

  (i) Walk forwards, backwards, sideways on the toes.

 (ii) Walk forwards, to the end, backwards to the start, and vice versa.

(iii) Walk forwards to the middle, or a mark. Turn round and walk backwards to the end. (At the turning point, ask the child to turn to the left or to the right.)

(iv) Walk forwards to the middle, or a mark. Turn round completely and walk forwards to the end.

1 Use the balancing plank. As children progress, tape bean bags and knotted ropes to the plank, and then cover it with mats to make an uneven surface.

2 Use the PE bench, broad side up. As children progress, use bean bags and knotted ropes as in 1 to make an uneven surface.

3 Use the PE bench, narrow side up. As children progress, wrap ropes round the rail to make the surface uneven.

4 Place bean bags under one end of the balancing plank.

5 Use two planks. Place bean bags under them, like this:

6 Place bean bags under two planks, like this:

7 Place bean bags lengthways under a plank, like this:

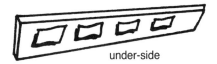

under-side

8 Slope the plank against wallbars or a trestle.

9 Place bean bags under the centre of the plank, like a see-saw.

10 Use a ladder on the ground. Walk, stepping between the rungs.

11 Walk along the rungs of the ladder.

12 Walk along the rails of the ladder.

MAINTAINING BALANCE WHILST AVOIDING OBSTACLES

Equipment needed
Large balls; large and small hoops; two blocks of wood, about the size of a house brick; bean bags; PE bench.

Preparation

Use two netball stands with a rope stretched between them, or a gymnastic beam. Place the balls in plastic bags and hang them from the rope or beam.

Activities

1 Suspend a ball at chest height. The child stands in a large hoop trying to maintain balance while avoiding the swinging ball.

2 As in 1, using a smaller hoop.

3 As in 1, standing in two chalked footprints.

4 As in 1, standing on two blocks of wood.

5 As in 1, standing on two bean bags.

6 Suspend a series of balls at various heights above a PE bench. Children walk along the broad side of the bench trying to avoid the swinging balls.

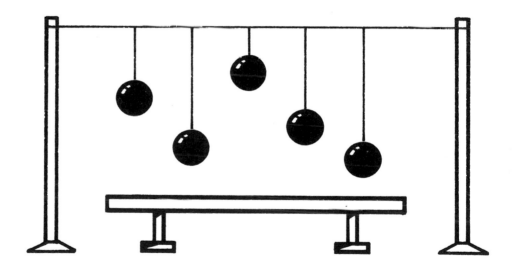

7 As in 6, using the narrow side of a bench.

Notes

(i) Children who have a balance problem may hurry across apparatus to complete the exercise before falling off. As a result, the effort and concentration required to feel balance is lost. The following list of activities will slow the children down and make them unconsciously work on the foot gripping and placement action, and take the care which is necessary. The activities also add a further challenge when required.

(1) Carry a large ball in each hand.
(2) Balance a bean bag on the back of one hand, then both hands.

(3) Balance bean bags on elbows, shoulders and head.

(4) Balance a quoit on the head.

(5) Balance a book on the head.

(6) Walk while balancing a bean bag on a table tennis bat.

(7) Walk while balancing a shuttlecock on a table tennis bat, first on its feathered base, then on its side.

(8) Balance an aerflo/tennis ball on a table tennis bat.

(9) Make up a variety of *sequences* on the bench such as: walk forward to the centre of the bench, turn half round to the left, then walk backwards to the end of the bench.

(10) Make up a circuit of a selection of the activities.

(11) Place PE bands along the equipment. Lift the bands with the feet and drop them off the edge of the apparatus.

(12) Throw knotted ropes, bean bags or balls to children while they are standing on (i) an uneven surface, (ii) a tilted surface, (iii) moving planks.

Balancing on one foot, hopping and skipping

In many assessment tests for gross motor skills, balancing on one foot, hopping and skipping figure prominently.

Teaching these activities very often presents problems to the class teachers because they are seen to be basic skills which all children should possess.

If a child cannot perform them no consideration is given to breaking down the skills so that they can be led up to in a progressive manner.

The three activities are related. Children who cannot balance on one foot have difficulty with hopping and if there is a problem with hopping, skipping very often proves difficult. Activities for the remediation of those gross motor tasks are taken singly but still graded from balancing on two feet, then one foot through to skipping.

All of the foot strengthening activities in programme 3 should be undertaken with pupils before and during the following activities.

Practising balance is more effective with bare feet as the 'grip' on the floor is better.

BALANCING ON ONE FOOT

Static balance on two feet

Equipment needed
Large and small hoops; cut-out footprints; blocks of wood about the size of house bricks; large bean bags.

Preparation
Suspend a ball from a beam or hook, using string, at chest height with the ball in a small plastic bag.

1 Stand in a large hoop, feet apart. Maintain balance while avoiding the swinging ball.

2 As in 1, using a smaller hoop.

3 As in 1, standing in two chalked footprints:

   (i) 10 cm to 15 cm apart

(ii) footprints side by side, touching

(iii) footprints, toe to heel.

4 As in 1, standing on the two blocks of wood, positioned as in 3(i), (ii) and (iii).

5 As in 4, standing on large bean bags.

Static balance on one foot

The child should be trying to achieve stillness in balance.

Equipment needed
Wooden blocks approximately 20 cm × 12 cm × 8 cm, or thick books.

Activities

1 Use two tables or desks, about a shoulder width apart. The child stands between them, feet slightly apart, one hand supported on each table. The child lifts each foot alternately as the teacher or partner places the wooden blocks, one at a time, under each foot in turn. This continues until the child is standing on two or three blocks, depending on ability level. Remind the child to 'grip' the blocks with the feet.

2 Initially the children look down until trust is gained. Then ask them to look straight ahead – tell them when to place their feet down.

3 Progressively delay the instructions on placing the foot, so that the child balances longer on one foot.

4 The child uses *one finger on each table* for support while performing activities 2 and 3.

5 The child uses *one hand on one table* for support while performing activities 2 and 3.

6 The child uses *one finger on one table* for support while performing activities 2 and 3.

7 The child puts a *hand on the wall* for support while performing activities 2 and 3.

8 The child performs activities 2 and 3 without support.

9 The child balances on either foot on request.

Moving into static balance on one foot

This is more difficult because the body weight is moving forward and the movement must be arrested on one foot without losing postural control.

Equipment needed
Hoops; wooden blocks.

1 The child takes giant steps into hoops.

2 As in 1, but ask the child to pause at each step.

3 As in 1, but ask the child to stop at each step for a count of *X* seconds. (Assess the child's ability to ensure they succeed with this.)

4 Use blocks in a stepping stone pattern.

(i)

⬜   ⬜   ⬜   ⬜
    ⬜   ⬜   ⬜

(ii)

⬜⬜⬜⬜⬜

Perform (i) and (ii) using the following instructions.

(1) Ask pupil to pause on each step.

(2) Ask pupil to stop on each step.

HOPPING

There are many activities involving *practising* hopping once the activity is established. The following activities help to teach the initial hop.
    Continue with the foot-strengthening exercises from programme 3.

Equipment needed
Sheets of newspaper.

1 Supported by the teacher or a partner, the child jumps on the spot on two feet.

2 Without support, standing on a sheet of newspaper, the child jumps once on the spot. Pull away the newspaper when the child is in the air. Show how the paper will tear if the child's weight is still on the paper.

3 Supported as in 1, the child balances on one foot, and hops on the spot, 1, 2 or 3 times.

4 Using a table or chair-back for support, the child balances on one foot on the newspaper. Ask the child to hop so that the paper can be pulled away.

5 Practise activities 3 and 4 on the other foot.

6 Hop, moving forward for a nominated number of hops.

7 Using chalk marks close together on the floor, hop from mark to mark. This should be practised until the hopping begins to look more smooth and fluid.

SKIPPING

It is important that the child has been through the activities on 'moving into static balance on one foot' before undertaking the following.

1 Chalk two footprints close together.
Balance on one foot on the first footprint – hop to second.
Repeat using the other foot.

2 Make four footprints together on either side of a line but close to it. Stand on one foot on the first footprint – hop to the next. Change to the other foot on the third footprint, and hop to the next.

This will be stilted at first, but will become progressively more fluid.

3 Mark the floor like this. Repeat activity 2 in a long line.

Again this will be stilted initially. Rhythmic voice patterns can be used to encourage fluidity of movement, then percussion instruments such as claves, beaters and tambours. Build up to a good 'skipping' rhythm.

P R O G R A M M E 5

Catching a ball

Catching a ball is another activity which appears in tests of eye/hand co-ordination, but the actual teaching of the skill often presents the class teacher with some difficulty. For the child, it is another status-significant skill; no-one wants to be the 'butter-fingers' of the class and the object of their amusement.

It is a skill which should be approached carefully and sympathetically. Some children are quite frightened of a ball coming towards them through the air, and are more inclined to avoid being hit by it than attempting to catch it.

If visual tracking appears to be the problem, attempt programme 12 first. The ball is 'captive' in this programme and children can work without fear of being hit by the ball.

While children are waiting to catch a ball, ask them to rub their hands together quite hard. The tingling sensation felt afterwards gives tactile feedback in the catching area of the hands. Tell them about this 'catching area'.

Before catching is attempted, making the hands familiar with the feel of a variety of sizes of ball is very useful.

Familiarity activities for the hands

Equipment needed
Balls of different sizes; bean bags, ropes, skittles, etc.

1 Standing feet apart, roll the ball in a figure of eight round the feet, using different parts of the hands – backs, fingers, palms, etc. – first in one direction then the other.

2 Sitting – legs bent, feet on the floor. Roll the ball gently under the knees from one hand to the other.

3 As in 2, but roll the ball under the knees and then round the feet – first in one direction, then the other.

4 As in 3, but roll the ball under the knees, round the feet, then round the back – in both directions.

5 Sitting – legs astride. Hold the ball near the ground in both hands – open the hands to release the ball. Try to get both hands back to the original position as the ball bounces up.

6 Sitting – legs straight, feet together. Place the ball on the ankles – raise the legs and catch the ball as it rolls down the legs.

7 As in 6, but first roll the ball down to ankles, then raise the legs and catch the ball as it rolls back towards the body.

8 Using different parts of both hands, guide the ball between and round an obstacle course made from bean bags, ropes, skittles, etc.

9 As in 8 using either hand.

Rolling and stopping a ball

Equipment needed

A large play ball; two PE benches.

1 Roll the ball – chase it and *stop* it.

2 Roll the ball – chase and run past it, crouch down and gather the ball in the hands.

3 Roll the ball against a bench or wall, gather the rebound in the hands.

4 Roll the ball along two benches placed a few centimetres apart to form a 'track'. Run to the end of the benches, crouch down and catch the ball as it falls off the bench.

5 (In pairs.) One child rolls the ball along two benches, placed side by side. The other child crouches at the end of the benches, catching the ball as it falls off the end.

6 (In pairs.) The children stand at opposite ends of a table and roll the ball to each other, catching it as it drops off the table.

7 (In pairs.) Slightly incline two benches placed with a space between them to form a 'track'. One child rolls the ball down the track, the other kneels on the floor to catch the ball as it rolls off the benches.

THROWING AND CATCHING

Using knotted skipping ropes

Preparation

Fold the skipping rope into quarters. Then tie a knot in the middle. This piece of equipment serves two purposes. To throw it, it must first be bunched in the hands – this has the same effect as rubbing the hands. When the rope is thrown up, it opens out and on dropping becomes tangled round the children's fingers, giving them *success in their eyes*.

1 Bunch up the rope in both hands, toss it in the air, and catch it in both hands.

2 As in 1, but toss the rope up with one hand and catch in two.

3 As in 1 and 2, alternating high and low throws (limit the height of the high throws).

4 (In pairs.) Toss and catch the rope.

Note

All the above activities can be done using 'button-filled' bean bags which are relatively easy to catch.

Using a variety of balls

Equipment needed

Start with a large ball, and use progressively smaller ones. All should be well inflated.

1 Kneeling, hold the ball at arms' length. Open the hands to drop the ball and 'clap' the hands gently on it as it bounces up. This encourages the *active* use of the hands, instead of waiting with them held in a basket shape hoping that the ball will fall into them.

2 As in 1, but gradually the hands, instead of meeting the sides of the ball, begin to form a basket *under* the ball.

3 As in 1 and 2, from a standing position.

4 As in 3, but throw the ball down gently to bounce.

5 Throw the ball up with two hands, and catch it with two.

6 Throw the ball up with one hand, and catch it with two.

7 (In pairs.) Throw and catch the ball, standing a short distance apart.

8 (In pairs.) Bounce the ball to partner for catching.

9 (Individually.) Throw the ball on to a wall, allow it to bounce, then catch it.

10 (In pairs.) Throw the ball on to a wall for partner to catch, allowing the ball to bounce first.

Throwing, striking and kicking a ball

Striking a ball with a bat and kicking a ball are activities recommended to improve hand/eye and foot/eye co-ordination. However, they are difficult to implement if a child cannot even follow the ball visually or make contact with it using a bat or a foot. If children cannot perform these activities they are unable to participate in age-related physical games. What are seen as status-significant skills are missing and once again self-confidence and esteem remain low for them within their peer group.

Activities for both underarm and overarm throwing are included in this programme because they establish the basic actions for striking a ball with a bat.

THROWING

Equipment needed
Bean bags; hoops; target shapes on wall.

Underarm throwing **Teaching points**

   (i) If the right hand is used, the left foot is forward for balance.

   (ii) The hand is drawn straight back.

   (iii) The delivery is smooth.

   (iv) On throwing, the hand 'follows through' towards the target.

   (v) Look at the target all the time.

1 Bowl the bean bag along the ground over progressively longer distances.

2 Throw a bean bag high into the air.

3 Throw a bean bag to hit a wall from some distance away.

4 Throw a bean bag to hit a big target, such as a door – better still, a double door.

5 Throw a bean bag to make it drop onto an upturned table.

6 Throw a bean bag to make it land on top of the table.

7 Throw a bean bag towards targets at various distances and heights, such as hoops on the floor and shapes on a wall. (The targets could have 'values' on them, and the child be encouraged to keep score.)

Notes

(i) Targets should be very large to give success, but it is the *action* which is important (see the teaching points). The targets can be made progressively smaller, and the distance to the target changed to make children aim, and to learn to judge the amount of effort needed to ensure the object being thrown reaches the target. This is known as the 'weight' of a throw.

(ii) Other skills can be developed at the same time: e.g. throw into a blue hoop; throw at a hexagon.

Overarm throwing

Teaching points

(i) If the right arm is used, the left foot is forward. The shoulders should be at right-angles to the target.

(ii) Point the left hand towards the target.

(iii) The right arm is bent, elbow pointing down, with the hand drawn back almost touching the right ear.

(iv) In the delivery, the right hand changes places with the left hand. The shoulders also turn to change places.

(v) The throwing hand finishes pointing to the target.

Activities

1 Throw a bean bag as high as possible. (This may be best done outdoors.)

2 Throw a bean bag as far as possible. (This too is best done outdoors.)

3 Throw a bean bag, as hard as possible, at a wall.

4 Throw a bean bag, as hard as possible, to hit a door.

5 Throw a bean bag, as hard as possible, at shape targets on the wall. (Keep score as before.)

STRIKING

Introducing the bat

The first step is to introduce a bat to 'guide' or 'dribble' a ball so that children can become familiar with holding the bat. If the ball is not fully inflated it is easier to control.

Equipment needed

Large inflatable ball; large sponge ball; table tennis bat; larger bat; bean bags; skittles, etc.

1 Guide a large ball around the area using the palm and the back of the preferred hand.

2 As in 1, using a table tennis bat in the preferred hand. Encourage the use of both sides of the bat to change the direction of the ball.

3 Using a large ball and bat, guide the ball to follow court markings in a gym, chalk lines or lengths of skipping ropes laid out in patterns.

4 Place a variety of equipment on the floor: bean bags, skittles, balls. The child uses a bat to guide the ball between the items without allowing the ball to touch them.

5 Mark a circle on the floor and a target on a bench or wall as in the illustration. The child stands in the circle and tries to strike a large sponge ball against the target. (The circle encourages the child to adopt the best possible stance for striking the target accurately.)

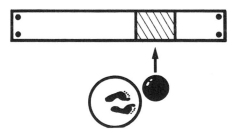

6 A partner or the teacher rolls the sponge ball to the child who strikes it back. The ball should be rolled so that the child does not have to move to strike it.

7 The child strikes a sponge ball continuously against a wall or bench.

Activities using balloons

Balloons are easy to strike and do not hurt. They are easy to 'track' visually as they float. When children are ready to hit them continuously they have time to get into the correct position.

Make up games for these activities to suit the ability of the children: for example, count the number of consecutive hits; number of hits in a given time; can they score X hits? Make sure the targets are attainable by the children.

When the children are preparing to strike the balloon underarm, ask them to hold the balloon in the *non-striking* hand in front and just above waist level. This hand acts like a tee in golf – the balloon should sit steady. The striking hand swings up and the non-striking hand is withdrawn simultaneously so that for an instant the balloon is stationary in the air.

When the children are preparing to strike the balloon overarm, the non-striking hands should hold the balloon, tee fashion, above and in front of the head. The non-striking hand is withdrawn as the striking hand is 'thrown' – this is how to explain it – at the balloon.

Equipment needed

Round balloons; rolled-up newspapers, table tennis bats, paper plates; small sponge ball.

1 Strike the balloon into the air, underarm, from a standing position.

2 Strike the balloon into the air, underarm, from a kneeling position.

3 Strike the balloon into the air, underarm, from a sitting position.

4 Strike the balloon, underarm, over a rope or through a suspended hoop or hit a target.

5 Repeat activities 1–4 using the other hand.

6 Strike the balloon with the back of the hands, fists, wrists, forearm.

7 Using these parts, repeat activities 1–5.

8 Repeat activities 1–5 using a rolled-up newspaper, table tennis bat or paper plate.

9 Repeat activities 1–5 using an overarm action.

10 Strike the *balloon* down to the ground to make it bounce as high as possible. Use an overarm action.

Using a small sponge ball

When the balloon programme is being performed satisfactorily, perform the same activities but holding a bat in the 'preferred' hand only and a small sponge ball. The preparation techniques remain the same.

The children can progress to the following activities, which can be done in pairs.

Equipment needed
Sponge balls; table tennis or short tennis bats; skittles.

1 One child bounces the ball to the other who strikes it underarm back to the thrower. The initial throw must be accurate.

2 As in 1, but the striker tries to hit the ball over a rope. The thrower is standing on the same side of the rope as the striker.

3 The striker hits the ball over the net to the thrower.

4 The striker, standing on a mark, returns the ball to the thrower, then runs to the side to touch a skittle, then back to the mark. The thrower serves the ball as the striker approaches the mark. (Have a few balls in a box beside the thrower so that he or she doesn't have to field badly hit balls.) This activity is to encourage the striker to make and then adopt a good hitting stance.

KICKING A BALL

The objective of the following activities is to give basic practice in foot/eye co-ordination, not coaching to play soccer. If the basic contact of foot to ball can be made satisfactorily the child will be encouraged to join in soccer games with friends and so gain more practice at kicking.

Familiarity activities for the feet These exercises are important. They allow children to learn what their feet can do with the ball.

Equipment needed
Large sponge balls or well inflated plastic play balls; small hoops; coloured PE bands.

1 Children should practise some of the running activities (programme 2).

2 Scatter boxes or schoolbags around the area. Children run between, around, and jump over the items without moving them.

3 Run around touching the items with nominated parts of the foot.

4 Scatter balls round the area and repeat activities 2 and 3.

5 Each child dribbles a ball from one end of the area to another, keeping it close to the feet with gentle touches.

6 Half of the group dribbles their ball round the area. The other half runs on the spot holding their ball. Then change over.

7 All dribble balls round the room, changing direction frequently.

8 Place a ball in a small hoop. The child moves round the hoop touching the ball with different parts of the feet, but keeping the ball in the hoop.

9 Place a ball in a coloured PE band. Repeat activity 8 trying to keep the ball in the band.

Kicking the ball from the ground

Children who cannot kick a ball very often have difficulty with balance. Giving a firm base to start with will help. They often find it easier to kick a ball coming towards them than one which is stationary. This is because they have not learned to establish a good base from which to kick. Use only the preferred foot throughout the activities.

Teaching points

(i) The kicker's arms are held out to the side for balance throughout the action.

(ii) The head is over the ball. The child looks at the ball all the time.

(iii) The non-kicking foot is alongside the ball.

(iv) The kicking leg swings back bent, swings through and straightens as it strikes the ball. The ball is struck with the laces of the shoes.

(v) The kicking leg follows through towards the target.

1 The child sits on a chair on one hip, with the kicking leg free and slightly bent. Place a ball at the instep of the kicking foot. Ask the child to straighten their leg quickly.

2 As in 1, but roll the ball accurately and slowly to the kicking foot. The child kicks it back.

3 As in 2, with the child kicking the ball as far as possible.

4 The child stands between two chairs (used for support) in a 'walk standing' position, the kicking foot at the back. Repeat activities 2 and 3.

5 Repeat activities 2 and 3 without support, paying attention to the teaching points.

6 Run to and kick a stationary ball as far as possible.

7 Run to and kick a stationary ball against a wall. Stop it when it comes back with the hands.

8 Run to and kick a stationary ball against big targets – a door, a large table on its side.

9 The child runs after a ball, rolled slowly forward, and kicks it before it stops moving, as hard as possible.

10 As in 9, kicking the ball at a large target.

11 As in activities 9 and 10, with the ball rolled from a variety of angles. (i) Kick hard and far; (ii) kick at large target.

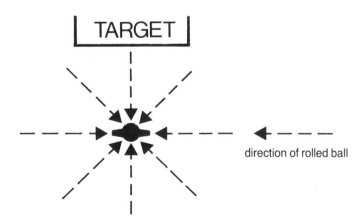

direction of rolled ball

**Kicking the ball
from the
hands**

Activities

1 The child sits in a chair, both feet together and slightly in front. The child holds a ball in two hands close to the kicking foot, drops the ball and kicks it as far as possible.

2 As in 1, kicking the ball as high as possible.

3 As in 1, kicking the ball to a partner.

4 The child stands in a 'walk standing' position, holding the ball slightly forward in two hands. The kicking foot is at the back. The child kicks the ball as far as possible.

5 As in 4, kicking the ball as high as possible.

6 Hold the ball in two hands – run forward and *stop* – kick the ball as far as possible.

7 As in 6, but kicking the ball as far as possible without stopping.

Jumping

A number of children find jumping quite difficult. In fact, some children cannot even leave the ground when asked to jump, particularly from two feet.

Children also need to have good postural control on landing to avoid stumbling and possibly hurting themselves.

Running jumps In these the child jumps from one foot and lands on two.

Equipment needed
Ropes; canes and skittles; large and small hoops; ball suspended in a plastic bag (see programme 4, p.37).

1 Run and jump anywhere in the area.

2 Run and jump over lines or ropes placed in the area.

3 Run and jump over a cane lying on the ground.

4 Run and jump over the space between two canes. Gradually increase the distance between the canes.

5 Repeat activities 1–4, trying to land on two feet without stumbling. (Emphasise how the knees should bend and the bottom should be lowered on landing.)

6 Repeat activities 2–4, trying to land in a large hoop without stumbling out of it.

7 Repeat activity 6, trying to land in a smaller hoop.

8 Run and jump over hurdles made from raised canes. The first height might be a cane supported by two books, for example. The height is gradually increased until the cane is supported on skittles.

9 As in 8, landing in a large hoop.

10 As in 9, landing in a smaller hoop.

11 Run and jump to touch a ball suspended above stretch height.

12 Run and jump to touch a ball suspended above stretch height, remaining still on landing.

Standing jumps   This can be a difficult jump for children – a standing jump with no run up whatsoever. With no forward momentum to help the child to leave the ground, their body weight must now be thrust upwards using muscle power alone.

The foot-strengthening activities from programme 3 should be undertaken first.

The *arm action* is very important in all of the following activities. It assists body lift.

Equipment needed
PE mats; cane; large hoop; PE band.

1 The child stands with feet a few centimetres apart, knees slightly bent with arms hanging by sides. The legs are straightened, raising the heels, to standing on the toes position. Simultaneously both arms swing forward and upward to almost stretch height. This is done on the spot. The child is *not* asked to jump.

2 Activity 1 is repeated a number of times with no pause between each movement. Instructions are given rhythmically: 'Swing up, and down!' 'Swing up, bend legs!' etc.

3 Repeat activity 2 four times but on the fourth count ask the child to swing both arms up as violently as possible. This may take the child off the ground. The word 'jump' is still not used!

4 Repeat activity 3 but on the fourth count ask the pupil to touch a suspended object with two hands. This is done with an encouraging command, 'Jump!' The suspended object can be a bean bag on a string hanging from a hook or beam, or tied to a cane which is held by the teacher. The height should be such that the child is able to touch the bean bag even with a very low jump.
The object to be touched should be slightly in front of the child.

5 Make a pile of four to six mats. The child stands on the edge of the mats, and then jumps down. (Emphasise the leg and arm action.)

6 Repeat activity 5, but hold a cane at the same level as the top mat and approximately 15 centimetres from it.

7 Repeat activity 6 with the cane held *slightly* above the level of the top mat.

8 Repeat activities 6 and 7, asking the child to land in a large hoop.

9 Jump from the *floor* on to the pile of mats.

10 Jump from the floor on to the pile of mats, to land in a band placed in a circle on the edge of the top mat.

11 As in 10, but then run across the mats, stop and jump from the mats into a hoop. Stand still on landing.

12 Jump from two feet to touch a suspended object.

13 Jump from two feet over a cane placed at an appropriate height for the child to succeed. Raise the cane as improvement occurs.

14 Standing long jump from a line for distance – measure this. The child is asked to beat that distance.

Miscellaneous activities

Equipment needed
Small coloured hoops and bands.

1 Place hoops close together in a line.

Taking off on two feet and landing on two feet, bounce from hoop to hoop along the line.

2 Place hoops in a line, separated by coloured bands.

Jump along the line of hoops and bands with two feet together *in* the hoops and one foot *on either side* of the bands.

3 Place hoops in a line with a *slight* space between them.

Repeat activity 2. This time the children have no band to guide them to get their feet apart.

4 Place hoops close together in a line.

Repeat activity 3. More care and control is now necessary.

5 Place alternately red and yellow hoops only in a line. Ask the children to jump with *two* feet landing in the yellow hoops and *one* foot in the red hoops.

6 Use yellow and red hoops, varying the pattern.

Repeat the instructions from activity 5.

7 As in 6, but the child is now asked to jump landing on two feet, between each hoop.

Body awareness through tactile feedback

The partner contests in this programme are planned for fun, while high-lighting particular parts of the body through very strong bodily contact. This makes the child more aware of the particular *body part being used* or the *direction of the movement*.

If the teacher wishes to *reinforce lateral dominance*, to establish use of the right hand for example, ask the child to use that hand for all the activities. If the aim is to *reinforce left/right knowledge*, encourage the child to use lefts and rights of body parts, e.g. feet, hands, side. If *body awareness* is the aim then the child should use parts of the body on both sides of the mid-line. It is also possible to *reinforce positional concepts* in this programme; e.g. face your partner; back to back; side by side.

When particular body parts or directions are to be taught by the teacher, go through the activities first, then question the children about these elements both *immediately* after participating and some time after the event. Useful questions are: 'Which hand were you using?' 'In which direction were you pulling?' 'Which part of your body was touching your partner?' And so on.

Do not physically move the children into position at first. Instead, by careful use of language, give step-by-step instructions. For example: 'Toe of the rear foot touching the heel of the front foot.' 'Hold your partner's right hand with your left hand.' If the children do not respond well, touch and name the parts you wish them to know as you put them into position.

Danish wrestle

Adopt the 'walk standing' position with the outside of the forward foot touching the same part of partner's. Grasp right hands. Pull or push partner off balance.

Chinese boxing
Stand facing partner. Grasp partner's right wrist with the left hand. Try to touch partner's face with the right hand.

Indian wrestle
Lie on the back, side by side, facing opposite directions. Link inside arms, with the hand on partner's shoulder. Raise the inside leg – try to hook partner's leg and pull them over. Change sides and repeat using the other leg.

Chinese tug-o-war
Stand back to back. Bend forward and grasp right hands between the legs. Pull partner to the opposite wall.

Hopping leg pull
Partners face each other, join left hands and grip each other's raised left ankles with the right hands. Each tries to hop and pull the other over a line or to a wall.

Armlock wrestle

Partners sit back to back with knees bent, elbows locked, one over and one under that of partner. Partners then try to force each other's upper body sideways on to the floor.

Leg lifting

Partners sit facing each other with feet astride, legs overlapping, each participant with one leg over and the other under that of partner; arms are crossed or the hands placed on hips. Each then tries to lift their partner's leg, at the same time keeping their other leg on the ground.

Crouch tug-o-war

Partners face each other in the crouch position, hands joined using the butcher's grip. With small jumps they try to pull each other over a line.

Arms-length touch

Partners stand, feet astride, facing each other but just out of reach. Each has one arm stretched out and the other behind back. Feet must not be moved! The object is to touch partner's head or nominated part of the body with the outstretched hand, without the partner doing the same. This can be a very useful balance activity. Feet positions can be altered as children become more proficient at the activity, for example

and

Balance tipple
Partners face each other ½—1 metre apart with their feet on a line or a floor-board. The toe of the rear foot touches the heel of the front one, both feet pointing directly forward. One hand is kept behind the back. The other is used open against the partner's open hand by hitting, pushing or feinting to make the partner overbalance.

Cock fighting
Partners sit on the floor facing each other with bent knees and arms clasped under the right thigh, both feet off the floor. With the left foot, children try to get their toes under their partner or to push them over. This is a good balance activity.

Wrist wrestle
Partners face each other lying on their front, with one arm behind the back. The children should be sufficiently close to allow hands to be grasped with forearms vertical and with about 15 cm between the elbows. The object is to force the partner's forearm backwards to the floor without raising the elbows or moving the body.

Hopping tug
Partners face each other, grasping right wrists and standing on left foot. On a signal they hop on this foot and try to pull their partner over a line or to a wall.

Elbow tug

Partners stand shoulder-to-shoulder, facing opposite directions with inner elbows linked and hands clasped across chests. The object is to pull sideways to get partner over a given line or to a wall.

PROGRAMME 9

Knowledge of left and right

This programme includes:
- **gross motor activities**
- **co-ordination activities**
- **left/right directional concepts**
- **visual perception**

The programme is best taught one-to-one, unlike the other programmes in this book. This is because other children in a remedial group may themselves have difficulties with left/right knowledge.

Many children are confused about the left and right sides of their own bodies and consequently are also confused about the directions left and right. This confusion creates difficulties for them in everyday life: they are baffled when asked to perform a specific task involving sidedness or to give directions. They may also experience stressful embarrassment.

There is a possibility that left/right confusion may contribute to reversal and inversion in writing. Teachers might like to note if use of this programme coincides with improvement in a child's writing of b's, d's, p's and q's.

The objective of this programme is to help children to internalise the knowledge of left and right, so that any response concerning these directions becomes automatic and instantaneous.

The method of progression, up to and including the activities using the suspended ball, should be as follows:

(i) Touch or indicate the body part or direction to be used or followed, giving the instruction at the same time. The child should not be given the opportunity to fail. *Correct guessing* must not be accepted!

(ii) Give the instruction without touching or indicating. For example, say 'Catch the ball with your *right* hand,' then pause before throwing the ball. The pause is to give the children time to organise their thoughts, and should eventually become zero. Ample verbal encouragement should be given.

(iii) The next progression comes by shortening the 'thinking' time still further, for example by throwing the ball and *then* giving the instruction.

Timing the children with a stop-watch where appropriate can also be useful. In hurrying to complete the timed tasks the need for speed may become the dominant feature of the activity for the child, enabling the teacher to observe if the selection of hand or direction is automatic and internalised.

Throughout the activities the use of tactile feedback is important to assist the child with identifying the body part or direction to be travelled but care must be taken as to how it is used. For example, if the right arm is *grasped* firmly to draw attention to it, any contact with the left arm should be different, perhaps *touched* firmly with a finger. This will help to avoid further confusion. The degree of firmness and length of contact should decrease as the child shows progress in internalising directional awareness.

The activities should be conducted in different parts of the room to prevent the child from using 'landmarks' in the room. If the activities are always conducted in the same place, the child may learn that by moving towards a certain door or piece of equipment, their response will be seen to be correct. This may delay internalising.

INITIAL ACTIVITIES

Equipment needed
Two bean bags; basket, hoop or netball ring.

Activities

1 Slipping step sideways, to left and right, on command.

2 Face another part of the room and repeat activity 1.

3 Repeat activities 1 and 2 with the child calling out the direction in which they are moving.

4 Hold a bean bag in each hand. On the command 'left hand' or 'right hand', the appropriate bean bag is thrown into a target, e.g. a basket, hoop or netball ring.

Catching in a cone

Equipment needed
Bean bag; two large cones made from stiff cardboard (holes may need to be cut in the apex of the cone to allow small children to grasp it easily).

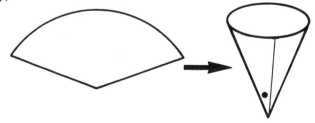

1 The child holds a cone in each hand and stands approximately 4 metres from the teacher. The teacher nominates which cone, left or right, is to be used to catch a bean bag, pauses, and *then* throws the bean bag. (Do not become concerned if the child cannot catch the

bean bag in the cone. The objective of this activity is to use the correct hand, *not* accurate catching. The cone is for fun.)

Take care in the early stages to throw the bean bag slightly to the left or the right of the child's mid-line, depending on whether the left or the right hand is nominated. This is necessary because some children experience difficulty with co-ordination if their mid-line has to be crossed to catch the bean bag. If the bean bag is thrown too far to the side of the mid-line, the child does not 'choose' a hand but simply uses the hand nearer the bean bag!

2 As in 1, but the teacher throws the bean bag *then* nominates the hand. The distance between the pupil and teacher is now important. The shorter the distance, the less time is available to the child to decide which hand has been nominated. Care, therefore, must be taken to allow the child to succeed.

3 As in 2 the distance being progressively reduced and the call delayed.

4 Repeat activites 1, 2 and 3, the bean bag being thrown directly at the child's mid-line.

5 Repeat activities 1, 2 and 3, the bean bag being thrown to the opposite side of the mid-line to the hand nominated. The child must now attempt to cross the mid-line to catch.

6 Repeat activities 1, 2 and 3, the bean bag being thrown to either side of the child's mid-line.

Using a suspended ball

Equipment needed
Ball suspended above stretch height from a hook or a beam; skittle.

1 The child runs and jumps to touch the ball with the nominated hand. As the child improves, the instruction 'left hand' or 'right hand' is progressively delayed.

2 Place a skittle 10 metres from the suspended ball. The child stands 15 metres from the skittle, runs to the right or left of the skittle on command, then jumps to touch the ball with the nominated hand. The commands are progressively delayed and the distance between skittle and ball progressively shortened.

Perception activities

Equipment needed
Small PE equipment; card shapes; large hoop; PE canes; chalk.

1 The floor is marked as in the diagram. A ball and bean bag placed on either side of the vertical line.

The child stands in the footprints, facing away from the equipment. On command the child turns and, one piece at a time, picks up the equipment and runs to place it in the same position on the other floor pattern. Initially the distance between the pattern is kept short so that the child does not have to retain the floor pattern image for too long a time. As the child progresses, the distance between patterns can be made greater.

2 Repeat activity 1 a given number of times. Count the number of correct responses. Next time the child tries to beat this score.

3 Introduce timing when the child is performing the activities well. The element of speed shows if the child is mastering quick retention of the pattern image.

4 Place two, then three pieces of equipment on either side of the vertical line. As progress is made, change the positions of the equipment frequently.

5 Use more complex floor patterns, and many pieces of equipment.

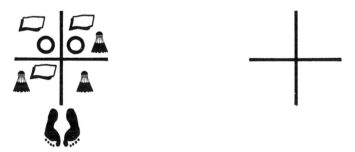

6 A variety of geometric shapes, made from card, can be used with the floor patterns. Start with each shape being the same colour. Progress to each shape being a variety of colours.

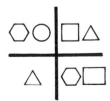

7 Use the following floor patterns. Place a large hoop in one of the quarters.

Proceed as in activity 1, the child placing the hoop on the appropriate quarter of the other pattern. As the child progresses, introduce elements of scoring and timing (as in 2 and 3).

8 Use the following floor markings and a large hoop.

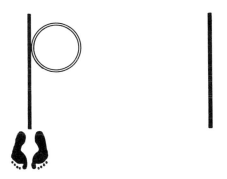

Proceed as in activity 7, the child now placing the hoop at the appropriate point on the vertical line. *Note* The hoop should be placed *only* as follows:

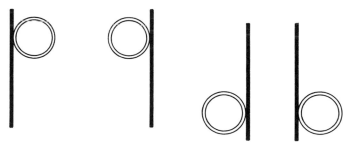

Increase the distance between the two vertical lines and introduce timing as the child progresses.

9 As in 8, but using a smaller hoop, then a rubber quoit.

10 As in 8, but the child *draws the circle with chalk* at the appropriate point on the right-hand pattern.

11 Similar activities can be set up using canes to make floor patterns like these, the patterns being placed on a line.

Throwing and catching

Equipment needed
Two hoops; bean bags.

1 Two hoops are placed as targets on either side of a line. The child faces the targets from a few metres away. A number of bean bags are placed at the child's feet.

The child picks up a bean bag in the *dominant* hand and throws underhand to the *nominated* target. For example 'Throw to the target to the left/right of the line.'

2 The child picks up a bean bag in the *nominated* hand and throws to the *nominated* target.

3 The teacher stands approximately 4 metres behind the child, and calls out 'right/left'. The child turns in that direction to face the teacher who then throws a bean bag. The child attempts to catch using *two hands*.

4 As in 3, with the teacher moving closer to the pupil.

5 Repeat activity 3, but the bag is thrown *before* the command to turn 'left/right' is given.

6 Repeat activity 5 with the distance between child and teacher being lessened and the call delayed.

7 As in 3, with *two* instructions given: first, 'Turn to the left/right,' then 'Catch in the left/right hand.'

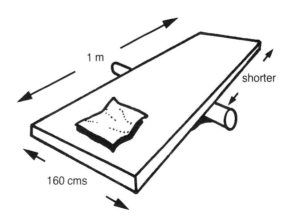

1 m

shorter

160 cms

Catching from a see-saw

Equipment needed

Broom handle; plywood 100 cm × 160 cm × 1 cm; bean bags.

Make a 'see-saw' like this. Put a bean bag on the low end of the see-saw.

Activities

1 The child stamps on the board with the nominated foot and catches the bean bag in two hands as it is propelled into the air.

2 As in 1, but with the foot and the catching hand being nominated, e.g. 'Stamp with the left foot, catch with the right hand.'

3 As in 2, except that the stamping foot is nominated *then*, when the bean bag is in the air, the hand is nominated.

4 The above activities can be given using cones to catch the bean bags.

P R O G R A M M E   10

Activities involving movement from left to right

This programme incorporates:

● **gross movements which are approaching fine**

The gross movements from left to right will help to establish this technique required for writing. Once children become proficient at working in this left to right pattern, they should be told that it is the same as writing on a blackboard or workbook.

Using sequence of targets

Equipment needed
PE bench on its side, flat surface facing the child, with the numbers 1–6 attached to it; a large and a small ball.

1 From behind a line roll a large ball to strike the numbers in sequence.

2 As in 1, with a smaller ball. It is not necessary for children to strike *every* number as long as they *aim* at each one and keep moving right.

Using quoits, bean bags and canes

Equipment needed
PE bench; rubber or card quoits; bean bags; cane or stick with slight point; box.

1 Lean quoits against a bench which is on its side. The children operate from behind a line, holding a stick or cane. Moving from left to right, they insert the cane into each quoit, lifting each one in turn, and dropping it behind the bench.

2 As in 1, but from a kneeling position inside a hoop opposite the centre of the bench.

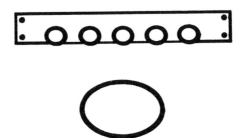

3 Place quoits on the top edge of the bench, overhanging it slightly. The children move the quoits as in activity 1.

4 As in 3, but from a kneeling position inside a hoop opposite the centre of the bench.

5 Place rubber quoits flat on the floor against the bench. The children move the quoits as in activity 1. (Note: card quoits cannot be used in this activity.)

6 As in 5, but from a kneeling position inside a hoop opposite the centre of the bench.

Notes

  (i) Initially the children can hold the cane or stick with both hands, but eventually they should perform the above activities holding the stick in their 'writing' hand only. When doing this, it is not necessary to hold the stick like a pencil!

  (ii) The teacher must assess the length of the stick to use. If the stick is too long, children may have difficulty lifting the quoit, particularly when one hand is used. When short sticks are used and children are operating from a hoop at the centre of the bench, ensure they are able to reach the extreme left and right quoits without difficulty. If rubber quoits are too heavy, quoits made from stiff card may be used in activities 1–4.

(iii) The stick should have a slight point so that children can manipulate it under the quoits in activities 5 and 6.

(iv) As children become more proficient at activities 1–6, place a box at the right-hand end of the bench and ask them to place the quoits in the box, one at a time, working from left to right. This simulates the writing process, where a positive action takes place from left to right before the hand/eye returns to the beginning of the line.

(v) Ask the children to increase their speed as they become more proficient.

7 Place bean bags along the top edge of the bench. The children hold the stick in the 'writing' hand and push the bean bags off the bench in a left-to-right sequence.

8 As in 7, but from a kneeling position inside a hoop opposite the centre of the bench.

9 Place bean bags along the top edge of the bench, and lean quoits against it. The children, kneeling in a hoop opposite the centre of the bench, push the bean bags off the bench in a left-to-right sequence and then return to poke the stick through each ring in a left-to-right sequence, without knocking them down. This simulates completing one line of writing, from left to right, then returning to the start of a new line.

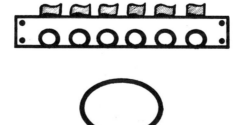

Using balls and cones **Equipment needed**
PE bench(es); balls of different sizes; hoop; cane or stick; box.

Activities

1 Use a bench with its broad surface uppermost. Place a large ball on its left-hand end. The children, holding a cane or stick in the writing hand, roll the ball along the bench surface from left to right, guiding it with the cane. They stop it at the right-hand end of the bench.

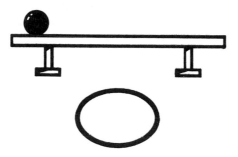

2 As in 1, but with a box at the right-hand end of the bench. Children perform the same activity but try to guide the ball into the box.

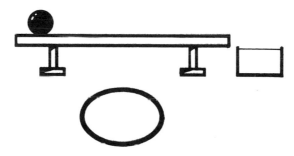

3 As in 2, but with another ball placed on the ground at the left-hand end of the bench. Children repeat activity 2, but when the ball drops into the box they immediately move back to the ball on the ground and manipulate it along the ground to the right-hand end of the bench, again using the cane. They stop the ball at the end of the bench.

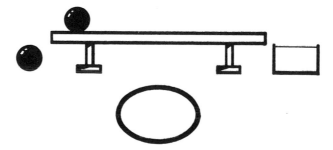

Notes

(i) If children find it difficult to keep the ball on the bench, use two benches a few centimetres apart. This creates a channel along which the ball can be guided.

(ii) As the children become more proficient, use progressively smaller balls.

(iii) A further progression is to ask the children to increase the speed of the activity. This should be done only when teachers have assessed by observation that the increase in speed is appropriate.

Visual discrimination

This programme includes:
- **gross motor work**
- **sequencing**
- **rhythm**

The activities use large geometric shapes (squares, circles, rectangles, etc.) and encourage children not only to identify the shapes but also to learn the shape names.

Shape sequences

Equipment needed
Large geometric shapes scattered over the floor.

1 Run in and out of the shapes. Stop at a given shape.

2 Skip in and out of the shapes. Stop at a given shape.

3 Hop in and out of the shapes. Stop at a given shape.

4 Slip in and out of the shapes to a given rhythm. Stop at a given shape.

5 Jump over the given shape.

6 Jump over *two* given shapes.

7 Stop at and roll over a given shape using a sequence of different types of rolls. For example, roll *forwards* at the first square, *backwards* at the second square and *sideways* at the third square. Then repeat the sequence.

8 Stop and make bridges, body shapes etc. above a given shape, trying to look at it all the time.

9 Perform a sequence of movements over two or three given shapes. For example, jump over a hexagon, roll over a circle and do a cartwheel over a square. Then repeat the sequence.

Notes

(i) For each activity, follow this sequence of instructing the children:
   (1) Show the given shape to the children.
   (2) Show and name the given shape.
   (3) Name the given shape without showing it.

(ii) It is beneficial to perform the running, skipping, slipping to an imposed tempo that is comfortable for the children, for example hand clapping, drum, tambour, claves, beating sticks. Increase or decrease the speed as the children are able to meet the challenge.

(iii) The above activities may be adapted for colour identification, and may use bean bags, hoops, skittles, quoits etc. The activities involving sequential memory are particularly suitable for this.

(iv) The *quality* of movement in rolls, cartwheels and jumps is not important in these activities.

A running game

Preparation
Place three different shapes in three corners of the room. Divide the children into three groups, each group standing beside a shape.

1 The children run, slip, skip etc. round the room. On a given signal they run to their own shapes.

2 The teacher holds up two shapes, and the children run to either of the two appropriate shapes.

3 The teacher holds up two shapes, and the children run to the shape which is *not* held up.

Notes

A greater number of shapes can be used if the teacher wishes. The sequence of instructions can still be (1) show the shape; (2) show *and* name the shape; (3) name the shape only.

Game using geometric shapes and colours

Equipment needed
Geometric shapes (one of each) inside large hoops placed around the room; coloured bean bags scattered about the floor, and within the hoops.

Rules

1 The children start by sitting in a line at the end of the room.

2 On a command, after receiving verbal instructions (see sample tasks below), they run as fast as they can to complete the task.

3 Bean bags picked up must be placed inside the hoops beside the nominated shape.

4 The winner is the child who completes the task and is first to sit down back at the starting line.

Sample tasks

1 Pick up *any* bean bag, place it beside a square.

2 Pick up a blue bean bag, place it beside a circle.

3 Pick up a blue and a red bean bag, place them beside a rectangle.

4 Pick up a blue and a red bean bag, place the blue bean bag beside a square and the red bean bag beside a rectangle.

5 Pick up a yellow bean bag, place it beside a circle, then pick up a green bean bag, place it beside a rectangle.

6 Pick up a green bean bag, place it beside a square, then pick up a blue bean bag from beside the square and put it beside a hexagon.

Notes

(i) The tasks given to the children can range from the simple to the complex, depending on ability and progress.

(ii) An element of *figure ground* work can be introduced if the bean bags in the hoops partially cover the shapes. This may happen accidentally as the children drop their bean bags in the hoops in an effort to complete the task as quickly as possible.

Visual tracking

A number of children have difficulty in visually tracking an object, let alone hitting or catching it.

In reading there is no 'cue' or object moving from left to right which a child can track. The words are stationary and it is only through experience that the left-to-right movement is established.

To children who are experiencing this problem, visual tracking can be introduced in a gross way and gradually fined down through progressive enjoyable activities to encourage them to reach the goal of not just hitting or catching objects, but left-to-right movement of the eyes across a page of writing.

The objectives of these activities are twofold:–

(i) To encourage the pupil to track objects with a view to striking or catching them. Head movements are quite acceptable for this.

(ii) To teach the pupil visual tracking from left to right. Initially head movement is acceptable but once the pupil is seen to track in this way quite easily, efforts should be made to encourage *no* head movement.

Visual tracking while moving

Equipment needed

Bundles of PE bands tied to ropes; bean bags; stick or cane; hoop; rubber quoits.

1 Moving backwards, the child pulls a rope to which is attached a bundle of coloured PE bands. The child looks at the bands while moving.

2 As in 1, but trying to make the bundle of bands follow court lines or chalk markings on the floor.

3 Scatter bean bags on the floor. As in 1, but trying to pull the bundle of bands between the bean bags without touching them.

4 (In pairs.) One child pulls the bands round the room. The other follows the bundle of bands, trying to touch it with his or her feet. (A simple challenge would be: 'How many times can you touch the bundle in thirty seconds?')

5 As in 4. The child pulling the bundle changes direction frequently. The chasing child, holding a stick or cane, tries to maintain contact with the bundle with the stick.

6 (In pairs.) One child pulls the bundle from left to right and then runs behind his or her partner back to the starting point (see diagram). The other child sits in a hoop approximately 2–3 metres from a wall, visually tracking the bundle from left to right until the bundle disappears from view. To view the bundle again the child must move head and eyes back to the left with no 'cue' to follow.

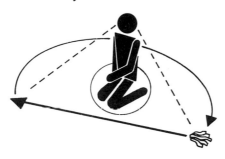

7 As in 6, but with a variety of bundles of bands behind the 'viewing' pupil. Each time the child dragging the bands goes behind his or her partner a different bundle is taken. When it comes into view the first child identifies and calls out the appropriate colour or combination of colours of bands in this new bundle. Bundles can be of one colour only or different combinations of colour, but should not include more than three colours in a bundle.

8 As in 7. The bands are dragged slowly. The child now stands in the hoop with several rubber quoits to throw at the bands as they pass in front.

Using 'swing ball' equipment

Preparation of equipment
Proper 'swing ball' equipment can be used in these activities. Alternatively, a tennis ball in a plastic bag tied with string to a netball stand can be used.

1 Stop the ball with one hand.

2 Collect the ball in a large plastic hoop.

3 Collect the ball in a smaller plastic hoop.

4 Collect the ball in a rubber quoit.

5 Catch the ball with two hands.

6 Stop the ball with a padder tennis size bat.

7 Strike the ball with a padder tennis size bat.

8 Stop the ball with a table tennis size bat.

9 Strike the ball with a table tennis size bat.

10 Strike the ball continuously, forehand and backhand.

Note

In activities 2, 3 and 4, use two hands initially to hold the hoops etc. Then to reinforce the use of the 'writing' hand once it has been established, ask the children to use it when stopping the ball or batting.

Using a suspended ball

Starting position
(i) The child lies on his or her back under the ball.
(ii) The ball, when stationary, should be suspended (from a beam or hook) directly above the chest, and at a height at which the child can stretch out and touch it.

1 Try to stop the swinging ball with one hand.

2 Touch the ball *gently* and try to keep it swinging.

3 Try to catch the swinging ball.

4 Strike the ball with one hand.

5 Strike the swinging ball with a padder tennis size bat.

6 Strike the swinging ball with a table tennis bat.

7 Strike the ball continuously.

Notes

(i) Encourage the child to keep his or her head still while tracking.

(ii) If there is head movement, place an object at either side of the head. The child will become aware of the head movement if the object is touched or knocked over.

(iii) Encourage the child to strike the ball *gently*. Otherwise the ball will move violently, making it difficult to track.

Visual tracking with body awareness

Activities

Equipment needed

Swingball, or improvised swingball equipment.

Stop ball with:

1 hand
2 palm of hand
3 back of hand
4 forearm
5 elbow
6 as above with head, shoulders, back, chest, etc.

Notes

(i) The teacher or another child can nominate which hand/arm to use (i.e. left or right).

(ii) The ball should be suspended at a height which will be suitable for the part of the body which is to be used, e.g. knee height for stopping with knees.

The rolling game

Equipment needed

A variety of balls of various sizes and colours; rubber quoits; toy cars and any small rolling toy which children can easily identify; two tables turned on their side approximately 2 metres apart.

Method

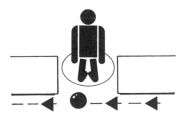

The child sits in a hoop a few metres away from the tables, as in the diagram. A ball, quoit, car, etc. is rolled from behind one table to the back of the other across the 2 metre gap. The child is asked to identify the toy, and to watch it until it disappears behind the right-hand table.

1 One at a time, roll large and small balls across the gap varying the sequence. Ask the child to describe the size of the balls.

2 One at a time, roll a variety of coloured balls across the gap. Ask for the colour.

3 One at a time, roll a variety of balls and toys asking the child to name the items.

Progression

1 Bring the tables closer together so that the child has a shorter viewing time and must concentrate on tracking from left to right to get the correct answer. Repeat activities 1–3.

2 Ask the child to lie on the floor facing the gap approximately 4 metres away. The child's head is supported and held still in his or her hands. Repeat activities 1–3.

3 Perform progressions 1 and 2 rolling the equipment increasingly faster.

4 Perform progressions 2 and 3 without holding the head with the hands but keeping the head still.

5 Use a table the right way up. Prop up two large pieces of cardboard, one at each end of the table. The child sits at the table, head held between hands.

A variety of small items is rolled across the gap between the cards, as in activities 1–3. Progressively narrow the gap and speed up the rolling.

6 Repeat progression 5 without holding the head, but keeping the head still.

7 Keep a score. Tell the child, that, for example, 10 items will be rolled. How many correct identifications can they give out of 10?

P R O G R A M M E 13

Activities for the 'writing' hand

Children who constantly produce very untidy written work and *who are going through the normal remedial processes to overcome this problem*, may also benefit from activities involving isolated hand movements.

Their problem may lie in the lack of hand strength. This may be observed in weak-looking, immature grips on the pencil. Hand-strengthening exercises in the form of not just flexion work, but strong hand extension and manipulative activities may be required. More control over the pencil will result.

In nursery schools and infant departments time is spent in gross motor activities but very few actual *exercises* are given for children's hands. They play with blocks, plasticine, use crayons, scissors, and attempt many other fine motor skills which require good hand control. Any strength work for the hands is incidental and usually of a flexing/gripping nature. Very little, if any, extension–spreading work is undertaken. Strength is required for good control of any movement, and to achieve strength both flexion and extension exercises are required.

The exercises could prove useful as part of a pre-writing programme before formal writing is undertaken.

Examples are shown on the following four pages of writing by children who undertook a course of hand exercises for approximately ten minutes daily for two months.

→

9/4/84

abcdefgghhijklmnopqr stuv wxyz

· There was a hamster in Johns.
classroom He was called Cheeky.
On Mondays Jon and Timothy.
looking after Cheeky They give Him.
Water and bits of carrot.

19/4/84

· Ther was a hamster in Johns.
classroom. He was colled cheeky.
on Mondays Jon and Timothy
looked after cheeky They give him. water and
bits of carrot.

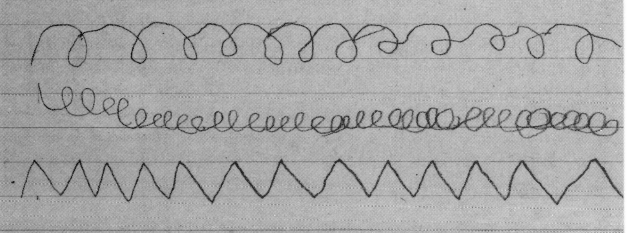

a a b c d e f g h i j k l m n o p q r s t u v w x y z

·There was a hamster in Johns
classroom H Wos called cheeky
On Mondays Johon and Timothy
looked after cheeky hhey gave him
water and bits of carrot.

9/4/84

Pupil 2

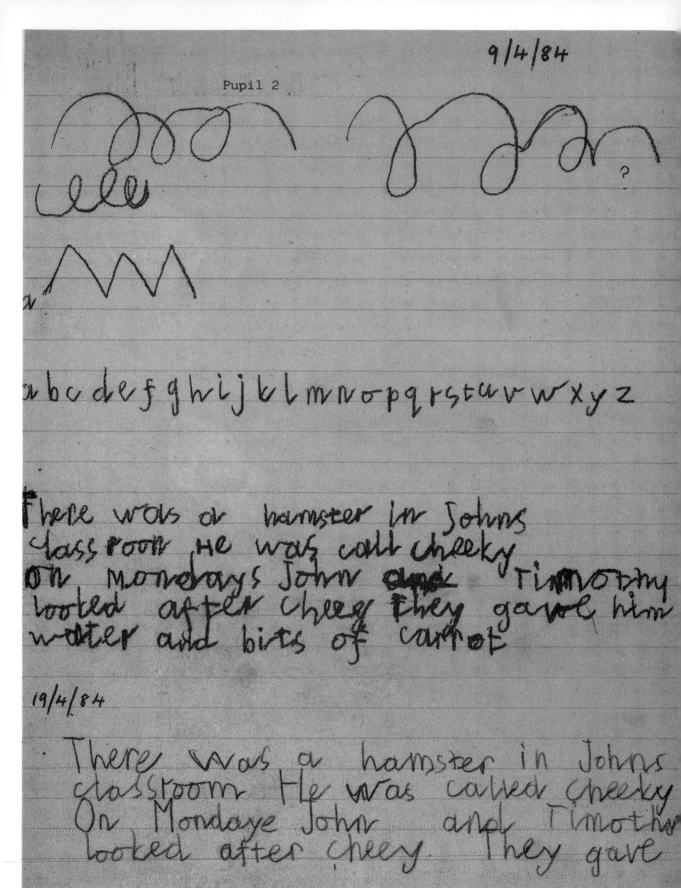

?

a b c d e f g h i j k l m n o p q r s t u v w x y z

There was a hamster in Johns
classroom He was call cheeky
On Mondays John and Timothy
looked after cheey they gave him
water and bits of carrot

19/4/84

There was a hamster in Johns
classroom He was called cheeky
On Mondaye John and Timothy
looked after cheey. They gave

12th June '84.

(handwriting practice patterns)

a b c d e f g h i n o p q
r s t u v w t x y z j k l
m

There was a hamster in Johns
classroom. He was called cheeky.
On Monday, John and Timothy
looked after cheeky. They gave
him water and bits of carrot.

Finger strengthening/ spreading activities

Activities

1 Sit with the palms of hands together, fingers spread. Keeping the fingers pressed together, push the elbows out and the heels of the hands down. Repeat a few times.

2 Sit with fingers interlaced. Stretch arms out in front of the body, pushing the palms of the hands forward away from the body. Repeat a few times.

3 Stand an arm distance away from a wall. Lean on the wall, with the hands flat on it. Keeping the arms straight, use fingers to push away from the wall to get to an upright position. As the child becomes more proficient, move the feet backwards so that there is a greater angle of lean against the wall.

4 Bunny jumps. Crouch down, place hands a shoulder width apart, and kick feet in the air. Ask children to keep their feet in the air as long as possible.

5 From a crouch position, with hands flat on the ground, try to touch a ball with the forehead without moving it. The ball is placed slightly in front of the hands. Start with a large ball, progressing to a tennis ball.

6 Cartwheels.

7 Modified crab walk.

8 Modified press ups, first on the hands, then on finger tips.

9 Modified chair dips. Kneel between two chairs, one hand on each chair. Push up with the hands to raise the body on to the toes.

10 Coffee grinder. Crouch down, with the hand used for writing on the ground to the side of the body. The child walks round the spread hand.

11 As in 10, but the free hand guides or bounces a ball as the child moves round.

12 (In pairs.) Wheelbarrows. The 'barrow' keeps fingers spread wide as he or she is guided along. This should be done for only short distances.

13 (In pairs.) Wheelbarrow wrestle. The child holding the 'barrow' tries to stand still. The 'barrow' tries to hand walk round the supporter and pull him or her off balance.

14 Two handed pushing using a board or tray.
Two children face each other in a walk standing position, arms outstretched, hands spread, holding the board between them. By pushing the board they try to push their partners backwards.

15 Squeeze a small sponge or squash ball, or a small ball of paper.

Notes

(i) Alternate extension and flexion activities.

(ii) Ask the children to shake their hands vigorously between activities.

Manipulative activities for the 'writing' hand

Equipment needed
Bandages.

1 A bandage is laid out across a table. The children sit at a table trapping the end of the bandage between the wrist of the 'writing' hand and the edge of the table. Using fingers only, they try to gather the bandage under the hand.

As the children progress the teacher can time them. This time is recorded and the children attempt to beat these times during subsequent attempts.

2 A bandage is laid along the edge of the table. The 'writing' hand is held above one end of the bandage with the wrist resting on the edge of the table. Using fast thumb movements only, the child tries to slide the bandage under the hand until the other end of the bandage is under the thumb; for example, if the right thumb is used, the bandage is moved to the right.

3 The child sits at a table and tries to move the fingers as if playing fast music on the piano.

4 The child sits with the heels of the hands together and fingers curled, finger tips apart. The child tries to touch corresponding tips one at a time, as quickly as possible.

Spinning activities

Before attempting these activities, the child should work on the finger strengthening/spreading activities.

Equipment needed

Hoops of various sizes; quoits; plastic balls; two ropes; PE bench.

1 Spin a large hoop.

2 Spin a large hoop. How many times can the child run round it before it stops spinning?

3 Spin two or more large hoops.

4 Spin two or more large hoops. Try to keep all the hoops spinning continuously.

5 Spin two or more hoops. Try to run between all the hoops before they stop spinning.

6 Repeat activities 1–5 using:

   (i) small hoop,

   (ii) rubber quoits,

   (iii) plastic balls of various sizes.

7 Spin three or more different pieces of equipment, e.g. quoit, ball, hoop. (See note (iii).)

8 (In pairs.) One child spins the equipment, the other runs round or between the equipment (as in 5). Try to score more 'rounds' than your partner.

9 Spin large/small hoops (as in 3) but try to keep them spinning between two ropes placed far enough apart to suit the ability of the child. This is to encourage greater control with the fingers.

10 Spin quoits or balls (as in 7), but on a bench top.

Notes

(i) Use the fingers of the dominant hand for spinning.

(ii) When spinning two or more times in a line, ask the children to perform the activities while moving sideways along the line from left to right.

(iii) After spinning three or more items, ask the child to repeat verbally the sequence of equipment used. Ask them to perform the same sequence.

(iv) Plastic play balls spin better than tennis or rubber balls.

(v) The largest hoop a child should use should reach only waist height. If they are any larger children have difficulty spinning them.

Establishing handwriting patterns

This programme incorporates:

● **gross motor activities which are approaching fine**

Handwriting movements across a page from left to right require fine motor skills and may present a child with some difficulty.

If a child is experiencing constant failure or producing very untidy work at such exercises as tracing to establish writing patterns, another avenue should be explored.

Gross motor work which approaches fine, using writing patterns from any handwriting programme, may assist the child. It should be presented as an enjoyable game.

Using benches, sticks, hoops and shuttlecocks makes the child feel that he or she is playing, but concentration is required to complete the tasks.

How the child holds the stick in one hand to perform the activities is unimportant. The aim of the activities is to establish the patterns and the left-to-right movement.

Equipment needed
P.E. bench; shuttlecocks; paper cups; bean bags; canes; hoops.

Activities

1 Side stepping from left to right *on* the bench, the child uses a stick to guide a bean bag or quoit between the bean bags or paper cups. If the child cannot 'see' the path between the bean bags, it should be drawn in chalk.

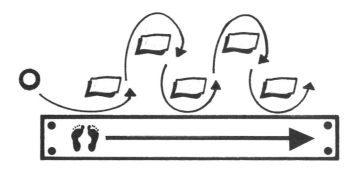

2 As in 1, but with the bean bags placed at more acute angles.

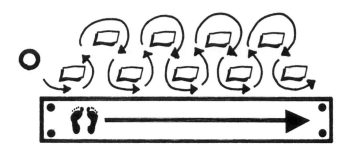

3 As in 1, but using canes. Keep the bean bag or quoit between the canes.

4 As in 3, but placing the canes closer together.

5 Put a small hoop inside a larger hoop. The child guides a bean bag round between the hoops.

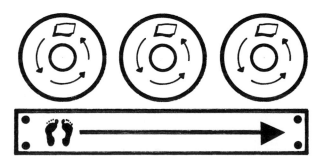

6 Place shuttlecocks or paper cups in a circle inside a hoop. The child guides a bean bag between the hoop and the shuttlecocks, trying to avoid knocking down the shuttlecocks.

7 As in 6, moving the bean bag in the other direction.

8 Move the bean bag continuously from left to right around the hoops.

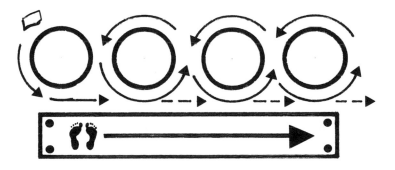

9 As in 8, using smaller hoops.

10 As in 8, using quoits.

11 As in 8, using bean bags.

Note

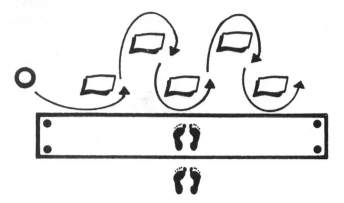

All the activities can be attempted from a standing position at the centre of the bench and working from left to right. For this, the children can either stand on the bench, or beside it and reach over it. This simulates sitting at the centre of a 'page of writing' and working from left to right to the end of a line of work.